Pushin' Up Daisies

PART A

The Personal Side of Funeral Service
Planning

PART B

The Business Side of Funeral Service
Saving

by Tracy Renee Lee, Funeral Director QCFH,
CEO QCFH, FDIC QCFH

ISBN: 978-0-9894447-5-0

ISBN-13: 0989444759

DEDICATION

This book is dedicated to my loving and supportive husband, G. Michael Lee.

Our marriage has been amazingly wonderful.

From the beginning, he always believed in my dreams.

HTTP://WWW.YOUTUBE.COM/WATCH?V=S641SPGR4HS

THE GRIEVING PROCESS

GRIEF IS A PAINFUL TIME IN OUR LIVES. SOMETIMES THE PAIN OF LOSING A LOVED ONE SEEMS UNBEARABLE. OUR EMOTIONS AT THIS TIME CAN GO AND COME WITHOUT WARNING. THE LENGTH AND INTENSITY OF GRIEF VARY FROM EXPERIENCE TO EXPERIENCE. THE RELATIONSHIP AND LENGTH OF TIME AND DEPTH OF LOVE ALL CONTRIBUTE TO THE SEVERITY AND LENGTH OF OUR GRIEF.

FEELINGS AND SYMPTOMS OF GRIEF

EXPERTS DESCRIBE THE PROCESS OF GRIEVING AND THE EMOTIONS OF GRIEVING IN DIFFERENT WAYS. THEY ARE COMMONLY LISTED AS SHOCK, DENIAL, ANGER, GUILT, SADNESS OR DEPRESSION, ACCEPTANCE AND GROWTH. THERE IS NO SET RULE FOR THE ORDER IN WHICH ONE MAY GRIEVE, NOR IS THERE A PRESCRIBED AMOUNT OF TIME THAT ONE MAY EXPERIENCE THE SEVERITY OF THEIR GRIEF.

SHOCK

WHEN DEATH COMES SUDDENLY, AS IN AN ACCIDENT OR MURDER, SHOCK IS GENERALLY THE FIRST RESPONSE PEOPLE EXPERIENCE. EVEN WHEN DEATH IS ANTICIPATED, THERE MAY BE DISBELIEF IN ITS FINALITY. A PERSON MAY FEEL NUMB, PASSING THROUGH THEIR DAILY RESPONSIBILITIES, WITHOUT AWARENESS OF WHAT IS AROUND THEM OR WHAT THEY ARE DOING. INDEED, MANY SURVIVORS REPORT THAT THEY FEEL OR REMEMBER VERY LITTLE DURING THIS STAGE OF GRIEF RECOVERY. AT THE SAME TIME, THEY MAY LOSE THEIR APPETITE OR EXPERIENCE CONFUSION.

DENIAL

SHOCK AND DENIAL ARE NATURE'S WAY OF SOFTENING THE IMMEDIATE BLOW OF DEATH. DENIAL CAN FOLLOW SOON AFTER THE INITIAL SHOCK. IT IS NOT UNCOMMON TO FEEL AS THOUGH YOUR LOVED ONE WILL WALK THROUGH THE DOOR, AS IF NOTHING HAS HAPPENED. SOME PEOPLE LEAVE BEDROOMS UNCHANGED OR MAKE FUTURE PLANS AS IF THEIR LOVED ON WILL BE A PARTICIPANT.

ANGER

ANGER IS A NORMAL RESULT OF GRIEF. ONE MAY FEEL ANGER TOWARD THE DECEASED FOR FEELINGS OF ABANDONMENT, TOWARD MEDICAL PERSONNEL FOR LETTING THEIR LOVED ONE DIE, TOWARD THEIR FUNERAL PRACTITIONER FOR UNEXPECTED EXPENSES, OR EVEN GOD FOR ALLOWING PAIN AND ANGUISH. ANGER MAY BE MILD OR RAGINGLY IRRATIONAL.

GUILT

FEW SURVIVORS EVER ESCAPE EXPERIENCING FEELINGS OF GUILT OR REGRET. "I WISH I HAD DONE MORE," "I WISH I HAD TOLD HER I LOVED HER THIS MORNING" OR "I SHOULD HAVE BEEN NICER LAST TIME I SAW HER" ARE WORDS THAT HAUNT MANY SURVIVORS. MOST PEOPLE ARE VERY CREATIVE IN FINDING REASONS TO SUFFER GUILT. "I WOULD HAVE DONE THINGS DIFFERENTLY IF I HAD KNOWN." EFFORT SHOULD BE TAKEN TO REALIZE THAT YOUR HISTORY WITH THIS LOVED ONE WILL NEVER CHANGE. PEOPLE WHO LOVE EACH OTHER SOMETIMES ARGUE, BUT IT IS NOT AN ARGUMENT OUT OF MALICIOUSNESS. MOST OFTEN IT IS A MOVEMENT TOWARD BETTER UNDERSTANDING AND COMPROMISE.

SADNESS

SADNESS IS THE MOST INEVITABLE EMOTIONS OF GRIEF. IT IS NORMAL TO FEEL ABANDONED, ALONE AND AFRAID. AFTER THE SHOCK, DENIAL AND ANGER OF DEATH HAVE PASSED, SADNESS AND SOMETIMES HOPELESSNESS MOVE IN. YOU MAY FEEL AS THOUGH YOU HAVEN'T THE ENERGY TO ACCOMPLISH EVEN THE SIMPLEST OF ACTIVITIES. CRYING EPISODES MAY SEEM ENDLESS.

DEPRESSION

In certain cases, sadness may move into depression. If the survivor is unable to move beyond this psychological and physical ailment, complicated grief becomes an endless battle. In such circumstances, professional counseling may be helpful.

ACCEPTANCE

Time alone will not heal grief. Acknowledging loss and experiencing the pain may encourage a survivor to overcome yearning. Accepting life without the lost loved one may give insight to the perspective of their new future. Acceptance does not mean forgetting. Acceptance is using ones memories to create a new life without the deceased loved one. Once acceptance has completed its course, new activities and relationships may develop.

GROWTH

Grief is a chance for personal growth. It is a time for rediscovery. Many people discover new hobbies, find new friends, develop new talents or join new organizations. Some people find new meaning in life by joining compassionate causes.

CONTENTS

Feelings and Symptoms of Grief

INTRODUCTION

You will outlive many people in your life for whom you will grieve deeply, loved ones whom you will miss terribly. The injustice, loneliness and pain will seem unbearable. Often you may feel that you cannot go on without them. You may wonder if there will ever be an end to your sorrow. You may feel that there is no hope. My dear friend, there is hope.

My purpose for writing this book is to help you navigate the confusing process of outliving those whom you love.

Death is hard on survivors. Emotions such as sorrow, grief, pain, loneliness, fear, regret, anger, hopelessness, helplessness, withdrawal and others, can be expected in most situations.

In other situations, there may be unexpected emotional challenges. These can be acute, subtle or nuanced emotions that vary with each unique situation. Take, for example, feelings that might be associated with the illness of a loved one that suffers the agony of disease; the unexpected sudden death of a loved one involved in an accident or murder; the miscarriage of a child not yet born, but anxiously anticipated. These are all deaths that carry a secondary element with which to cope. Each of these carries grief-filled experiences for the survivors.

As you read through this book, I hope you will understand that there is no easy way through the experience of sharing someone's death. There are, however, things you can do to prepare for your loved one's death that will relieve you of many of the burdensome tasks associated with the ending of someone's life. These preparations will give you some amount of control in a situation that seems out of control.

Accepting, adapting, anticipating and meeting these challenges will free you and prepare you to tackle the necessary road to recovery with greater ease and comfort.

If you have the fortune to know in advance of an expected death, take this time to get things in order. Although you may not look on this opportunity as good fortune, in actuality, it truly is.

You have the advanced knowledge and time to resolve past conflicts. You have the ability to forgive, reconcile and settle ill feelings. You can decide and implement estate issues. You have the time to notify others to establish precious moments before this loved one is out of reach. In so doing, you will have protected yourself, from a measure of undue and unwelcome stress when the dreadful day of death arrives.

After you have put a plan into action to offer everyone the opportunity to correct any issues with your future decedent, the next step is to pre-plan your funeral needs.

At this point, whatever the case, whether you are planning your funeral or the future funeral of a loved one, your course of action should be the same.

Explore, evaluate and pre-plan your funeral needs. Doing so will save you time, money, stress and heartache.

Pre-planning is an act of love for yourself, for those whom you love and for those who love you. It is a gift worth giving and a gift that will be appreciated when death occurs.

This book is written to help you through the planning and preparation of pre-planning a funeral. Many people do not pre-plan a funeral because they are intimidated or afraid of the process.

My goal is to help you overcome these fears by offering

information and facts that will enable you to realize that funeral planning is inevitable and one way or another, you are going to do it.

Let us do it the easier way, in advance of need, when decisions can be made without overwhelming stress, armed with solid knowledge so that you will not be vulnerable to those who might take advantage of you.

A funeral director's job is to protect her client by sharing information that is pertinent at the end of a loved one's life. She has prepared and expanded her knowledge to guide you toward the decisions and qualified persons that can protect you legally, emotionally and financially. The passing of a treasured loved one creates an unwelcome vulnerability. The survivor's ability to think clearly, understand the consequences of certain decisions and to function at their usual level of competency is greatly impaired. These reactions are common. Your body is coping with the extreme circumstances of death. It has compromised your ability to comprehend fully, what is happening so that the extreme pain of this loss will not crush you.

It is imperative that you have a trustworthy funeral director to guide you through this confusion so that once you are experiencing the consequences of your decisions; they are consequences you can live with, rather than ones you suffer from or regret.

In order to bring this book to you, I have invested over a decade of preparation. During this time, my family has invested unwavering support in me, seven days a week, twenty-four hours a day. It has been a family mission. It has been our family goal.

We have invested all that we have and all that we are, into this endeavor. Extended family put up collateral, loaned us equipment, showed up to help paint, carry heavy tile, run electrical wire, move thirty foot long oak church pews out of an old downtown church and into a storage barn. Of course, those thirty-foot oak church pews had to be moved out of the storage and into our chapel, once it was built. We cut down trees, leveled ground, filled in holes, ran water lines, ran electrical lines, built cement signage, helped plant flower beds along with earthwork to complete our first funeral home. We have directed traffic, parked cars, played the piano, sang hymns, made sandwiches, carried lemonade by the gallons, dressed in kilts and learned to play bagpipes.

We have done so much more, but we do not have the time or space to list it all. The difficult part has not even begun. We must work through years of continual investment into this business before we will ever see a penny come out of it. Our initial one million dollars is merely a drop in the bucket compared to what we will have invested when the much-anticipated day of profit transpires.

It has been a hard and long road, the traverse of which we have lived and loved from the onset. Unless you are a funeral home owner and the funeral director in charge (FDIC, yes it is a legal and regulated title in the funeral industry), you will never be exposed to this much specialized knowledge of the funeral business.

Few people neither see the need for nor want this much knowledge and experience of the funeral business, but most would like to benefit from it.

It is through this book, and the advice within its pages, that you will have a greater understanding of the ins and outs of the funeral business. You will understand the laws that govern burials and cremations. You will better understand the procedures, policies and covenants that help regulate the industry of dealing with the dead and their survivors.

In short, the more you know, the better off you will be, and you will be positioned to endure a better funeral experience.

How do you get the most out of this book?

When you were young, you were probably scolded for grabbing a crayon or pencil and writing or marking up a book. You didn't know any better. You were a child and saw the book as an object of paper on which to express your creative childhood self. It is not a bad practice to keep books in pristine shape. It is a good practice to refrain from defacing or destroying books. Books contain knowledge. Good books contain good knowledge.

There is an old story about two sisters who married at about the same time. Their mother, wanting to give them each a special gift, bought for each, a brand new Holy Bible.

In not too many years, both daughters had young families and were doing all they could to raise their children as best as possible.

The first sister, cherishing the gift from her mother, put the holy book way up out of reach, so that it would not get damaged. This was a reasonable thing to do as she had rough and rowdy boys.

The second sister would use her copy of the holy book to read to her children, even when it seemed like they were not paying attention. Once a page was torn out, and one of the boys used a marker to draw a boat and a pony on two of the other pages.

By the time these two sisters were old, the first sister had a book in as good condition as the day it was printed. She also had kids who had been to jail and had hard lives.

The second sister's Bible was barely more than tatters, but the words and wisdom of its pages were now written in her children's hearts.

Like the books referenced above, this book is just a tool for your use. It is here to serve you. I would hope that you would do as I have done with many of my most-cherished books.

A book is only worth what you get out of it. It has long been my personal practice to read with a highlighter or pencil in hand. I underline ideas and passages, take notes, highlight facts and earmark pages for future reference.

You are about to embark on an adventure that will save you tons of stress, tons of heartache, and tons of money.

If you prepare for the worst day of your life before it happens, your suffering and recovery time will be greatly diminished.

You will still grieve, but you will not be taken advantage of, and you will be better prepared to face life as a survivor.

My goal is to help you have a better funeral experience by arming you with knowledge, understanding and preparation.

THE INFORMATION IN THIS BOOK IS PURLY INFORMATIONAL.

FOR LEGAL ADVICE,
please see an attorney.

FOR FUNERAL ADVICE,
please see your preferred funeral practitioner.

PART A

THE PERSONAL SIDE OF FUNERAL PLANNING

ALL FUNERAL PLANNING IS A DEEPLY PERSONAL HUMAN EXPERIENCE. THIS SECTION OF PUSHIN' UP DAISIES WILL HELP YOU UNDERSTAND THAT ALTHOUGH FUNERAL SERVICE IS A BUSINESS, IT IS AND SHOULD ALWAYS BE SERVICE BASED.

CHAPTER 1

A BETTER FUNERAL EXPERIENCE

A BETTER FUNERAL EXPERIENCE

The question one might ask at this point is,

"What is a better funeral experience?"

If you have ever attended a funeral you most likely know they are not always happy occasions, and they do not always end well. Often, funerals are filled with hurt feelings between siblings, between extended family or between blended-families. Some of these issues may be headed off simply by following that "Golden Rule" you learned when you were in grade school.

The Golden Rule

"Do unto others,

as you would have others,

do unto you."

Easy enough to say, but not always so easy to follow.

When a death occurs, it seems every past family issue must somehow mysteriously reappear. This is not the best timing.

As a funeral professional, I have only experienced one funeral where there was absolutely no evidence of disagreements or ill feelings between anyone. After extensive surveying and interviews of my colleagues in the funeral industry, I am saddened to report that there was only one other account of a funeral that had no evidence of internal family bickering, battles, politics and strife. Only one out of dozens of funeral directors recounting hundreds, if not thousands of funeral events such as viewings, wakes, memorials, burials and cremation services could recount a trouble free event.

Emotions run high at funerals. If someone has an issue or unfinished business with anyone else in attendance, it is likely to rear itself at this time. Stress can be high at a funeral. This is not a good time to try to correct a previously unsettled problem. In many states, it's illegal to take a firearm to a funeral for this very reason. Tension and tempers run high, and people are in emotional and compromised states of mind.

A word of advice from the funeral director...

"If you have unfinished business with someone at a funeral, hold it back. I PROMISE there will one day be a more suitable occasion for addressing your issue.

If you follow this advice, you will have a happier life and everyone at the funeral will be grateful to you, hold you in higher esteem and appreciate you for exercising the self-control they know they so sorely lack themselves. You will be heralded as the coolest cat ever, and revered as a greater person."

These actions of self-control will of course yield a better funeral experience. However, the better funeral experience with which I intend to help, is much more than this.

The better funeral experience of which I speak will come from following my advice. This advice, which I now happily and gladly share with you, is a product of my years of personal and professional observation, training and experience in the art of funeral direction.

CHAPTER 2

PHILOSOPHY OF KINDNESS

Principle 1

Philosophy of Kindness

Amma Essie Zylks Harville
(Tracy's beloved grandmother)

My grandmother always told me,

"Kindness, like a boomerang, always returns."

Her principle of life...

is our philosophy of funeral service.

My American roots extend back to the beginning of our glorious nation. My early American ancestors moved to this country and settled on the Southeastern seaboard and into the deep southern United States.

After the revolutionary war, bit by bit, my family left the east coast and moved to, for the greater part, Louisiana and Texas. As generations of births came and went, my great grandfather was born in Cass County Texas. My great grandparents married and my grandmother was born. She was a tough lady born during a tough time. She grew up on a sugar cane farm during the Great Depression. Her work ethic was founded on honesty, virtue and hard work.

I learned my work ethic at the feet of my beloved grandmother, Amma Essie Zylks Harville.

Principle 2

An American Work Ethic

When I was a little girl, my grandmother Amma was a chicken farmer. She would take me out to her commercial chicken house, and we would gather eggs together. Once we had the lot gathered, we would take them into the sorting house and wash and measure them for market. It was a small country operation, but it kept us in food and clothing.

It was during this process that my grandmother would share with me the stories of her life, experiences of the Great Depression, the advent of telecommunications and of the amazing speed differences of traveling by automobiles compared to horse and buggy.

At a very young age, I became keenly aware of my appreciation of the modern conveniences of which my grandmother spoke. Her strong belief of earning one's keep was passed from her generation to mine.

As a young woman, I married a career military man and thus found myself out of the southern United States during his military tenure. Once he retired, we moved back to the area of my birth, and once again, I find myself surrounded by my family and friends.

Sadly, however, my grandmother passed away while visiting us when we were stationed at Marine Corps Base, Camp Pendleton, California. Her death and the experience of preparing her for travel back to the area of her birth was the life-changing experience that motivated me to become a funeral director.

My grandmother was the kindest woman I have ever known, and for those who knew her, this statement is no surprise. She was nurturing, incredibly loyal, hard working and caring by nature. Her desire to instill these qualities into the generations that followed her is my gain.

Principle 3

Honesty with your Fellowman

My grandmother spent her daylight hours working either in the family garden, which kept us all in food or in the chicken house which provided for our monetary needs.

As I would sit in the chicken house with my grandmother, she would recount stories of growing up on a sugar cane farm and being very poor during the great depression. Her stories would have moral value and in listening to them, I would learn life's lessons.

She praised the virtues of being thrifty, sincere, hardworking and charitable along with many others. One of her particular lessons was that of honesty.

My grandmother put a special emphasis on honesty. It was her opinion that if a person were dishonest, he or she would not be worth his or her weight in dirt.

She taught me,

"Honesty is the best policy in all you say and do."

She was a shining example of virtue, and I have missed her every day since her death.

Principle #4

Improve each Generation

"It is the responsibility of every generation to ensure that those that following are better off than their own."

This is a principle of truth.

If you are not engaging in ensuring that your children have better opportunities than you did and that your grandchildren have better opportunities than your children did, society is doomed to failure. It is through the experience of life that we pass to our descendants the ability not to repeat our mistakes.

You have heard the adages, "History repeats itself", and "Those who don't know their history are destined to repeat it."

Do your family a grand favor.

Break that cycle.

Through the power of active parenting, engaging grand parenting, and for the lucky few, hands-on great grand parenting, make those years count.

CHAPTER 3

THE PURPOSE OF FUNERALS

Purpose of Funerals and Why Should I Have One

The answer to this question is very simple if one studies history any at all. The family is the very smallest form of organization in human society, yet it is the strongest one. Without strong families, society begins to break down. In countries without strong families, we begin to see failures in school, work, business, cities and states. We see wars, famine, abuse of persons, abusive governments, gang violence and the list goes on.

Families are Forever

The funeral and the ceremonies that accompany it are very important. A funeral provides a place for family and friends to gather for support. Modern funeral homes are designed with families in mind. Your comfort and inclusion are paramount in every aspect of your loved one's funeral service. With that in mind, chapels have big screen TV's and surround sound, offering each person attending preferred seating. Overflow seating arrangements are designed to accommodate the special needs of those in attendance. Often, reception services are available as well.

Each of these elements is designed to ensure that your funeral needs are met, as well as the needs of your family and friends. Psychologists and other experts agree that funerals are for the benefit of the living, those left behind, and those who must reconstruct their lives without the companionship of the deceased.

Experts have declared that the survivors (those left behind) must openly and realistically face the fact that death has occurred. The funeral and its accompanying ceremonies are the sole opportunities to accomplish this vital realization. Families that forgo the funeral experience find that grief recovery can be very complicated and greatly extended. The funeral service is a way of saying good-bye and letting the healing process begin.

It is the event that ushers in the commencement of recovery. Without this important ceremony, families and survivors are at an increased risk of complicated grief. Complicated grief sets survivors up for depression, insomnia, loneliness, reclusiveness, illnesses and even premature death.

In my experience as a funeral director, I believe funerals are vital to health, grief recovery and continued life.

Families that do not understand the profound importance of familial bonds across their generations, often suffer great psychological discrepancies, in multiple aspects of life. The failure to bond and love one's relatives often leads to an inability to develop these important skills in other relationships. These basic relational instincts and talents must be learned and developed under the protection of unconditional love. If not, successful lateral relationships will result in failure though out life. One's ability to obtain happiness, self-esteem, success and love will be greatly diminished.

Through the successful cultivation of strong families, greater success and happiness will inherently develop. Greater sorrow and grief will al be experienced upon the loss of beloved family members. An opportunity to gather and offer love and support to each other is crucial at this juncture. The funeral is the sole event offering the opportunity to say goodbye to the esteemed loved one by those who loved and cared for him or her.

CHAPTER 4

WHEN DEATH OCCURS

When Death Occurs

The loss of a loved one can be very difficult and confusing. During this stressful time, it is important to understand the decisions that must be made. Funeral Directors are licensed, experienced and caring. They understand this is a heartbreaking time for you and your family. A good funeral director will help support and guide you through the most-difficult days to follow. They are there to help ease your burden, protect your well-being and provide you with sound information.

If you find that your funeral director fails to provide you with these essential requirements, ask for a different one, or consider using a different funeral home.

What To Do First

Death at the Hospital

When a family member enters a hospital or nursing home, and life is at a critical stage, the staff will usually inquire if final arrangements have been made. If the answer it "no," they will ask if there is a preference for a certain funeral home over any other?

It is always best to notify the hospital or nursing staff upon admittance of your funeral home preferences. In so doing, you can concentrate on final moments with your loved one rather than trying to make important decisions as precious life is slipping away.

Once death has occurred, the hospital staff will wait until you inform them that you are ready for the funeral home staff to come to the hospital.

At this point, the hospital staff should call the Funeral Home of preference and give them notice that their services have been requested.

Some families want the funeral home to come right away while others would like extra time before their loved one is taken away.

Under Hospice Care

If in the care of a hospice program, notification will be made in a similar fashion by a hospice staff member. Even if your loved one has been admitted into the hospital, unless they have been discharged by hospice, they remain under the rules of hospice. In other words, a qualified hospice member will pronounce death and notify the funeral home listed in the patient's medical record.

The same holds true if your loved one is in a nursing home. Once death has occurred, or just prior to death occurring, hospice will be notified by the nursing staff that death has occurred. The hospice nurse will then travel to the place of death in order to pronounce the time of death. Be aware that the hospice nurse will announce the time of death as the moment that he or she pronounces it. Your loved one may have died hours ago, but until hospice pronunces death, officially, death has not occurred.

Once death has been verified and pronounced, hospice will ask the family members in attendance if they need extra time before the funeral home is called.

When the family is ready, the hospice member will summon the funeral staff, and they will come and take the family member into their custody.

If your family member is dying at home, hospice will be keeping a close watch on him or her. If death occurs while hospice is not at your house, just give them a call, and they will come right away. As before, if you need extra time, they will give your family a few minutes to a few hours before they call the funeral home.

In all other Situations

In all other situations, a family member or person with the deceased should notify emergency personnel immediately. If you do not know the direct phone number to your local police department, 911 gets them notified in an efficient manner.

Grab your phone,

Diall 911

Tell them the address

and that you have a dead human being there with you.

The 911 operator will ask you additional questions, but at this point the police and emergency services will be dispatched.

The additional information she is gathering from you is evidentiary. It is also, for the safety of the police, yourself and the emergency personel.

Unexpected or Sudden Death

When death is unexpected or sudden, the family is in a state of shock and unprepared for loss. In this circumstance, one needs to call in emergency personnel immediately. At this time, you might also find it very convenient and comforting to call in a close family friend or a clergyman.

If your family member has had an accident, emergency services may already have been called to the scene. If you happen upon your loved one and they are unresponsive or in obvious need of medical assistance, call 911 immediately.

In certain cases, your loved one will be transported to the hospital or to the medical examiners office. Most likely, an autopsy will be ordered. An autopsy is generally ordered when death is sudden, the decedent was not under the care of a physician, or questionable circumstances exist.

If this is not the case, emergency personnel will inform you that the services of a funeral home are necessary. You will be asked for a preference and most often, dispatch will notify the funeral home that they are needed.

One should realize that the funeral home personnel will not be there within 10 minutes as the emergency personnel were. At this point, the emergency has subsided and the situation has moved from urgent to serious.

The funeral home personnel must gather documents and follow procedures inorder to protect the family and decedent. Unlike emergency personnel, funeral personnel are not at work at 3:00 AM. They are most likely on call and in their beds asleep. They will need a few minutes to wake up, shower, get dressed, drive to the funeral home, gather the necessary paperwork, transfer into the first call vehicle and then drive to your location. All of this takes time.

Once they arrive at your location, there will be questions that must be answered and paperwork that must be signed. If the funeral director is unable to be there and other funeral home staff has come in their stead, they will be unable to speak with you about anything relavant. Most likely, they will merely hand you a card, if they have one with them, and ask you to call the funeral home in the morning to schedule an appointment to come in for an arrangement conference.

Federal regulations impose silence on these funeral personnel unless they are licensed funeral directors. They are unable to answer any questions you may have. You must speak with a funeral director to obtain any information at all.

If the funeral director was unable to be there to accept custody of your loved one, he or she will call you within an hour or so and ask you a few simple questions. These questions will be related to you services. The funeral director needs to know as soon as possible about your plans for burial or cremation. This information will protect and preserve you loved one in order to accomplish a pleasant and legal, final persentation for your family and friends.

By the time your funeral personnel arrive, you may feel as though an eternity has passed, or you may feel as though they arrive too quickly. Time moves at a different pace when one has suffered loss and no one knows whether it will move at warp speed or at a snails pace. If your funeral personnel arrive before you are ready to release your loved one into their custody, just ask them for a few more minutes. Most likely, they will be happy to allot you ample time before they gather your loved one into their protection and leave for the funreal home.

The funeral home is there to serve you and they have been educated to this end. Whatever your immediate needs are, they will most likely be willing to accommodate them. Funeral personnel understand the physcological impact of grief, and they will try to accomplish the transition of custody as seamlessly as possible.

What to do Second

At this very difficult time, it is a good plan to gather the family together, and to call upon your clergy for support. Once your funeral director arrives, she will prepare your loved one for custodial acceptance.

Custodial acceptance is the transfer from your protection over your loved ones body into the custodial protection of your funeral director. Your funeral director is now the legal custodian of your loved one, and she will need to gather information directly related to the wishes of last disposition.

As the next of kin, you will be called upon to provide preliminary instructions for the immediate care of your loved one and to sign instructional documents.

Instructional documents are legal documents instructing the funeral home in the immediate care of your loved one. These documents will be authorizations for the funeral home to either embalm your loved one or cremate your loved one. These documents are very important as time makes a difference in the appearance and preservation of your loved one. These documents are also binding you to the expenses for such services.

After the initial business of how to prepare your loved ones body has been completed, the funeral home will leave with your loved one and begin preparations according to your instructions.

Your next duty as next of kin is to go to the funeral home to finalize the details of services and final disposition. You will be selecting merchandise, deciding who will participate in the ceremonies and providing vital information for legal documents. You will also provide payment for your selections and services at this time. Be prepared to enter into legal negotiations and binding contracts at this conference. The funeral home will have already incurred expenses on your behalf, and they will expect and require payment.

It is critical that you have your wits about you at this time. You must get some rest if you can. The next time you meet with your funeral director, you will be making decisions that will affect the estate of your loved one and details of his or her services and final expenses.

It is easy to get lost in all of the details and planning of funeral services and estate transference. I would caution you to be very aware and to be cautious before making any major decisions. At this time, concentrate on only those decisions necessary to carry out final disposition.

Things to bring to the Funeral Home

Vital Information

Vital information is comprised of the legal details of one's life. They include lineage, both ancestors and descendants. Female lineage is recorded under maiden history, so be sure to know the decedents mother's maiden name. Birthdates, birthplaces as well as your loved one's social security number will be collected. In some cases, counties of birth are necessary data. Citizenship, work history, education and race are collected for statistical purposes.

Clothing for the Deceased

It is sometimes easier to choose a casket if you know what your decedent will be wearing once they have been prepared for casketing. It is also more convenient to bring these clothes with you to the funeral home so that you do not have to make an extra trip to bring them back. Although you may not have realized it yet, you are going to be extremely busy and near exhaustion. Eliminating extra trips will help preserve your strength for urgent and pressing matters over the next few days.

Payment

Whether you will be utilizing insurance policies or paying cash for your services, you should be prepared to pay in advance of services being rendered. The funeral home will be expensing major purchases on your behalf, and they need to have guaranteed funding before they can move forward on your behalf.

Pictures

When you arrive at the funeral home for your initial arrangement conference, you will need to have a dedicated picture for your loved one's newspaper obituary. You will also need pictures for the printed program, any keepsake printings and for the memory movie.

Digital images are the most convenient for the funeral home's production staff. In many cases, the funeral home will be forwarding these images to other vendors who specialize in photographic arts. In order to get them emailed and back in time for services, digital is the only option. If the pictures are not originally from a digital format, you can scan the images and take them in on a digital jump drive or CD.

Musical Selections

Some families are very traditional and only request religious hymns at their loved one's services. Other's prefer recorded popular music. If you have certain music you would like at the services, be prepared to either provide it or pay a fee for the use of copyrighted materials.

As before, digital recordings are more easily utilized by the funeral home. If you are going to have a live performance, be sure to inform the funeral home so that they can make the appropriate accommodations for the performers.

Names of Program Participants

Many families already have their program planned and may want to produce their own personalized funeral service folders. This is, under less stressful circumstances, a wonderful idea. One must realize however, that a funeral is not a stress free circumstance. During funeral week, the family is quite often over stressed with many details. Accommodations for friends and family, suffering great anguish and grief, meal preparation, extra laundry, etc are just a few examples of added work and stress that must be endured at this time. Although printing programs at any other time may not be a burden, when it comes to funeral week, that may very well not be the case.

Program details

If you do not have your funeral program pre-planned, your funeral director will begin helping you organize your order of service. She will ask for your clergy's name and phone number, and various details in order to plan the funeral service. She will need the names and phone numbers of the person who will be delivering the eulogy, the invocation, the benediction, the reverential or pastoral remarks, as well as the names of your vocalist and her accompanist.

If you will be utilizing recorded music, she will need the title, arrangement and artist you prefer. Keep in mind, recorded music is copyrighted and therefore subject to royalty fees. In playing recorded music, you may fall under legal regulations and be obligated to pay the required royalties to the recorded performing artist.

Insurance and Pre-Need Policies

As payment is due before services are rendered, you will need to bring your insurance and pre-need policies with you to the arrangement conference.

Your funeral director will verify that the insurance is intact and have you sign an assignment form so that the insurance may be relied upon for payment.

Bear in mind, most funeral homes utilize a third party processor on insurance policies. The third party processor will advance the funeral home the insurance funds so that the funeral home may cash advance your service expenses. This third party processor will attach charges for the advancement of funds. These charges will be added to your funeral expense and will come out of the insurance policy, along with your other funeral expenses.

What to do after the Funeral

The days following a funeral may be confusing and difficult to bear. This is a time that others might be relied upon to take care of tasks that might otherwise require your attention and action. A neighbor might offer to collect and sort your mail; a family member might offer to mow your lawn for the next few weeks. These are simple tasks that you might be accustomed to handling, but over the next few weeks, might seem overwhelming or unimportant.

Allowing others to carry some of your burdens can be a great gift to yourself and to those who wish to serve and help you through what may be one of the most horrific experiences of your life.

After your loved one has been laid to rest, there are a number of things you must do. The following is a list of some of these tasks. You may find that there are many more tasks than those listed. I suggest you begin a notebook of things you need to do. Once you have accomplished them, check them off your list. This will help you accomplish and keep yourself organized, during a time that is generally difficult to remain so, and function at your normal capacity. Your ability to function at maximum effectiveness may be greatly compromised through your grief recovery experience. This notebook will help you maintain your organizational skills by creating a central location and tracking method of what tasks need to be done, what tasks have been completed and what tasks need consideration and scheduling.

Although this may seem tedious and unnecessary in the beginning, once you have begun moving completed tasks off your list, you will be grateful you are not committing time and efforts into doing tasks you have forgotten that you have already completed. It also allows you to relax, knowing that as you think of additional tasks, they are written down. This takes away your worry over forgetting and trying to recall them when your brain seems over tired, heavy laden and perhaps at times, confused.

TO DO LIST

- Send acknowledgment cards
- Transfer real estate properties
- Notify insurance companies and file claims
- Apply for appropriate benefits
- Notify bank, stockbroker and credit card companies that a death has occurred
- Notify Department of Motor Vehicles and transfer titles
- Notify Attorney/Accountant/Tax Consultant
- Notify utility companies

CHAPTER 5

FUNERAL PLANNING

Funeral Planning

One of the most caring and loving things you can do for your family is to pre-arrange your funeral. This takes away the burden of planning your funeral at a time when they are under great stress and experiencing bereavement. If you have already planned your funeral and made payment arrangements, your family will have a great burden lifted from them at a difficult time. Your funeral home of choice should take the time to make each service as unique and personal as you are. And, they should do this while honoring budget limitations. They should also accept most existing prearrangement plans and insurance policies from other funeral homes.

A little note about insurance and Pre-Arrangement funds. These funds function similarly to a checking account. If you open your checking account in San Diego, California and then go on vacation to Miami, Florida, you can use your monies from your bank in California to pay for your vacation needs in Florida. If you needed to, you could write a check at your hotel or the grocery store. Your check would draft the money from your account into the account of the hotel or grocery store. They would provide the goods and services you need, and your bank would pay them on your behalf.

The same holds true with funeral funds. The funds are yours, to be used on your behalf. The funeral home only receives funds if they provide the goods and services. If you purchase a funeral fund in San Diego, California and then move to Miami, Florida, a funeral home in Miami can accept your funds just as well as the funeral home in San Diego. Instead of writing a check though, you would sign an "Assignment" or "Change of Beneficiary." These two documents function similarly to a check would from your checking account.

In this case, these documents would transfer your funds from one place to another. It is very simple and very common.

Before the Arrangement Conference

Before coming to an arrangement conference, there are bits of information that you should gather to help things run smoothly for you.

The following list contains suggestions of some of the basic information your funeral director will be required to gather on your behalf.

Vital Statistics

Name of Decedent

First, Middle, Last (Maiden)

Current Address:

Street, City, State, Zip

Sex

Ethnicity

Citizenship

Birth Date

Birth Place

City, State, County, Country

Father's Name

First, Middle, Last

Living or Deceased

Current Spouse's Name

Place of Residence

Mother's Name

First, Middle, (Maiden)

Living or Deceased

Current Spouse's Name

Place of Residence

Marital Status

Married, Divorced, Widowed, Single

(If a person has been married previously and is currently divorced, they would not qualify as single. They would qualify as divorced.)

Name of Spouse

First, Middle, Last (Maiden)

Living or Deceased

Place of Residence

Social Security Number

Highest Level of completed Education

Employment History

Usual Occupation

Field of Work

Military Service:

Branch of Service

Service Dates, Entry and Exit

DD214

Obituary Information

Spouse

First, Middle, Last (Maiden)

Living or Deceased

Place of Residence

Parents

First, Middle, Last (Maiden)

Living or Deceased

Spouse's Name

Place of Residence

Brothers,

First, Middle, Last

Living or Deceased

Spouse's Name

Place of Residence

Sisters

First, Middle, Last

Living or Deceased

Spouse's Name

Place of Residence

Adult Children,

First, Middle, Last

Living or Deceased

Spouse's Name

Place of Residence

Minor Children

It is unusual to name minor children in an obituary. This practice is in observance of safety. Therefore, your funeral director will most likely only ask for a number of minor children for the newspaper notice.

Grandchildren

It is unusual to name minor children in an obituary. This practice is in observance of safety. Therefore, your funeral director will most likely only ask for a number of minor children for the newspaper notice.

Living History

A history of the decedent's life for the obituary may be lengthy or brief. The lengthier the history, the more expensive your obituary will cost. Customarily, the funeral director will compile the obituary and have you proof it. Once everything is correctly recorded, your funeral director should email the obituary into the news publications of your choice for an estimate. In so doing, you will not be surprised by the billed amount.

Obituary or Eulogy

If you have been asked to give the eulogy at a service, you should realize a few very important facts.

You have been given a great honor. You need to take this request seriously, and earnestly prepare for its delivery. The family of the deceased is counting on you to help them remember the very best moments in their loved one's life.

There is a very distinct difference between an obituary and a eulogy…

The Obituary

An obituary is a biographical list of facts about a person who has recently passed away.

It is usually written by the funeral director from the vital information he or she has gathered at the arrangement conference.

It is printed in the newspaper.

It is often printed in the funeral folder or laminated on bookmarkers.

If is factual and rather impersonal.

Example

John Smith

February 1959 – January 2014

John Smith, born February 1959, died January 2014.

John is precede in death by his parents Howard and Ella Bell Smith. He is survived by his wife Etta Burns Smith; son Harry Smith and wife Georgia of San Diego, CA; daughter Sara and husband Roger Brown of Escondido. CA; brother James Smith of El Cajon, CA; and two grandchildren.

Visitation will be held Wednesday, January 8th at 4:00 PM at Miles Funeral Home in Vista, CA. Funeral services will be Thursday, January 9th at Miles Funeral Home. Interment will immediately follow at Greentree Cemetery.

The Eulogy

A eulogy is written and delivered as a speech.

It contains personal experiences and tells the life's story of the deceased.

It is generally delivered at the funeral/memorial service by a personal friend or relative.

It is reserved for a very dear and trusted person and should be prepared with great care and consideration. Family and fiends are relying on this person to tell the story of their loved one life. The eulogy can make the difference between a mediocre and an impactful funeral experience..

A very kind and considerate act is to professionally print the Eulogy and present it to the next of kin after the interment service.

GUIDE TO WRITING A EULOGY

A eulogy or tribute to the deceased should be written by a family member or friend. It is a special part of the funeral service.

When one is called upon to compose and deliver the eulogy, one sometimes wonders where does one start with this important task?

A eulogy can simply be a recollection of personal memories shared by family members, friends or work colleagues. It can be as simple or as creative as the presenter wants it to be.

A creative presenter can deliver a spectacular life story with recollections of hilarious and touching moments from his/her memory. They can also include stories of particular importance to the family.

If it is decided that a simple eulogy is preferred a chronological account of the decedent's life may be recounted with dates and places from various events of importance. This eulogy will cover such areas as childhood, adolescence, adulthood and in many cases old age, stopping along the way to make reference to and expand upon:

- Employment

- War service
- Marriage
- Children
- Grandchildren
- Favorite holiday destination and anecdote
- Hobbies/past times/travel
- Club memberships, etc.
- Sporting interest
- Interest in – books, music, films, television
- Favorite expressions/nicknames
- Who was he/she? In just a few words, describe him/her.
- What will you miss most and always remember?

Helpful Phrases

- Our shining star
- Beloved and loving Wife/Husband
- Our lives were enriched by his/her love
- Much loved and loving
- Always remembered

- A friend sadly missed
- Loving memories
- Peacefully resting
- Always in our hearts
- Fond memories
- Rest in peace
- Rest peacefully in God's care
- Treasured memories
- Simply the Best
- The gates of memory never close
- Forever with the Lord
- Until we meet again
- Always treasured and remembered
- Safe in the arms of Jesus
- A patient sufferer at rest
- Cherished memories
- Beyond the sunset
- May his/her dear soul rest in peace

- Lord keep and always remember him/her
- Loved and always remembered
- Peace, perfect peace
- Dearly loved
- Sadly missed
- Gone home
- The righteous live forever
- At rest
- Time passes, but memories remain
- Thy will be done
- The long day closes
- Now the day is over
- Old soldiers never die; they simply fade away
- To know him/her was to love him/her
- The memory of you shall remain in my heart forever
- Your love and kindness will stay with us always
- Gone fishing
- Life's journey is over

- To live in the hearts of those we love is not to die
- Memory is the treasury and guardian of all things
- Loved and respected by all
- We mourn his/her passing – but celebrate his/her life
- Loving memories will always keep him/her near
- Sadly missed and often thought of
- Forever in our hearts

CHAPTER 6

FUNERAL ETIQUETTE

ETIQUETTE

Although common sense and good discretion are always the best guides to proper funeral etiquette, a few principles apply.

Condolence Visits

Close friends of the bereft family, if possible, should visit the family's home to offer sympathy and assistance as soon as they possibly can after learning of the passing. This is sometimes called the "Condolence Visit." It may include helping with food preparation and childcare. The visit can take place anytime within the first few weeks of death. It may be followed with one or more additional visits, depending on the circumstances and your relationship with the family.

Share Memories

In addition to expressing sympathy, it is appropriate to relate to family members your fond memories of the deceased. In some cases, friends and family members may simply want you to be a good listener to their expressions of grief or memories of the deceased.

In most circumstances, it is not appropriate to inquire as to the cause of death.

Showing Respect

It is customary to show one's respect at the visitation by viewing the deceased if the body is present and the casket is open. You may wish to say a silent prayer for, or meditate about, the deceased at this time. In some cases, the family may escort you to the casket.

Visit with others

The length of your stay at the visitation or funeral/graveside service or reception is a matter of discretion.

After visiting with the family and viewing the deceased, you can visit with others in attendance. Normally there is a register for visitors to sign and the family appreciates it if you would sign it. Most funeral homes provide free online memorial pages that include a guest book where tributes may be posted.

Children at a Funeral

At a very early age, children have an awareness of and a response to death. At the parent's discretion, children should be given the option to attend the funeral service.

Your funeral director can advise you on how to assist children at this vulnerable time in life. He or she might also provide specific information and literature on helping children cope with death.

In my book,

Children and Death,

I provide detailed information on grief work that parents can implement to help children have a healthy adjustment and recovery from the death of a loved one. I focus on age appropriate perceptions and understandings, and provide methods to help you overcome your fear of helping young children overcome their grief. You should also be aware of the child's needs at the funeral. If they seem afraid or upset, it might be a good time to consider leaving.

Be sure to prepare your child for what he/she should expect. Explain to them the traditional ceremonies before they happen. If your child begins to act poorly at the services they are attending, you might consider taking a break to another part of the building or if the child is out of control and causing disturbances, leaving might be a better solution.

A child's reaction is difficult to predict, so be aware and take proper actions if you decide to bring them to the funeral home or cemetery.

My book,

Someone Has Died,

is a children's book, written with illustrations to help your child understand what is happening. It also addresses funeral etiquette at a child's level.

Conservative Dress

As with other aspects of modern day society, funeral dress codes have relaxed somewhat. Black dress is no longer required. Attire should always be respectful toward the family and this loved one.

Some obituaries will direct the guests as to attire. If you are unsure, err on the side of respect.

Flowers, Donations or Cards

You can send flowers to the funeral home prior to the funeral or to the family's residence at any time. In some cases, flowers may also be sent to the church. Flowers are not sent to Jewish synagogues or Catholic churches.

If the family has opted for limited services, the funeral home will not accept flowers and gifts on their behalf. These items should therefore, be sent to the family's home.

Charitable gifts in memory of the decedent are often made, particularly when the family has requested gifts be made in lieu of flowers. The chosen charity should be noted in the obituary along with the address and accepted method of donation.

The Funeral Home's website will direct donors to the proper charity or organization. The family is notified of the gifts by personal note from the donor or by the charity itself. In the latter case, the donor provides the family's name and address to the charity at the time the gift is made.

It is usually acceptable to send flowers even when the obituary or death notice states, "in lieu of flowers, please make a contribution to..." Flowers at the funeral service not only add warmth and life to a somber event, they are a tangible tribute. They let the bereaved know, visibly, how much their loved one touched the lives of others.

You could also send flowers after the funeral. It is a thoughtful gesture to send flowers several weeks after the funeral service to show the bereaved that you are thinking of them, and they are not as alone as they might feel.

Send a note or card. Even if you don't send flowers or make a charitable contribution, a note or card to the decedent's family expressing your thoughts of the deceased is a welcomed gesture, especially if you weren't able to attend the funeral.

It is important to let the bereaved know you are thinking of them. Even if you are only an acquaintance, sending a card is appropriate. The card should be in good taste and in keeping with your relationship with the family of the deceased.

A personal note of sympathy is very meaningful and very much appreciated. Express yourself openly and sincerely. An expression such as "I'm Sorry for your personal loss" is welcomed by the family and can be kept with other messages. It can even be meaningful to send a card a couple of weeks after the funeral.

Online Tributes and Guestbook

Many funeral homes offer online condolences and guest books for each of their families.

Even if one has sent a card, it is a very kind gesture to enter a condolence on the decedent's online memorial page. These pages are available to the decedent's family and friends indefinitely. These condolences will bring continued comfort to the decedent's family, friends, co-workers and acquaintances long after the cards and well wishers have vanished.

Etiquette for the Family

The family should acknowledge the flowers and messages sent by relatives and friends. When food and personal services are delivered, the family should recognize these thoughtful acts and send a note of gratitude. Even the services of the pallbearers should be recognized by sending a note of thanks. The funeral director may have acknowledgement cards, which can be used by the family.

When a contribution or gift is received from a person well known to the family, a short personal note on the acknowledgement card expressing appreciation for a contribution or personal service received is nice, i.e.

"Thank you for the beautiful roses. The arrangement was lovely."

"The food you sent was enjoyed by our family.

Your kindness is deeply appreciated."

In some communities, it is a practice to insert a public thank you into the newspaper. The funeral director can assist you in this task.

Sample Thank You Notes

• Note One

Words fall short of expressing how much your care package touched my heart and brought a smile to my family's faces. You have always been by my side for so many of life's side-journeys.

• Note Two

If you live long enough, there will come a time when you will experience the death of someone close to you.

At such a time, the love and support of family and friends are absolutely invaluable. It helps us heal. And, for that loving support, we are forever grateful.

• Note Three

Thank you so much for all the support you have offered me and my family and me during this difficult time. I know it could not have been easy, and I really appreciate your friendship.

• Note Four

I know that you loved (name of deceased), and count his recent passing a great loss. Please know that we greatly appreciated the (name food item) you brought by.

Thanks so much for thinking of us at this very difficult time.

- ## Note Five

We have been through so much together over the years. I don't think I could have survived this past week without your love and support.

- ## Note Six

My family and I would like to thank you for your support and generous donation to my mother's charity fund. You were a great friend to her over the years, and I know she loved you very much.

- ## Note Seven

Thank you so much for attending my mother's funeral and for the beautiful arrangement you sent. Our family appreciates your support.

- ## Note Eight

There are simply no words to express my heartfelt thanks for the sympathy you have extended toward our family during this time of loss. We are deeply grateful to you.

- ## Note Nine

Dear Reverend,

- Thank you for your spiritual counsel and services at the funeral of my mother. Especially at times like these, your guidance is so appreciated.

- ## Note Ten

Thank you for serving as a pallbearer. You are a true friend. Your contributions to the service were a tremendous help. I appreciate your kindness.

CONSOLING

Death is difficult for everyone. Even if you have experienced a loss in the past, it may still be difficult to console someone close to you who has suffered one recent loss.

Below are some tips and suggestions on how you can help the bereft.

Helpful Suggestions

- Say "I'm sorry."
- Give them the opportunity to talk about the deceased.
- Allow them to share their memories.
- Use the deceased person's name.
- Validate that grieving is normal.

Ask your friend how you can help

Not so Helpful Phrases

- I know just how you feel.
- Time heals all wounds.
- Aren't you happy he's in heaven?
- You're lucky your baby's in heaven with God.

- Be thankful he was not aware at the end.

- Things will get back to normal in a month or two; you need to get on with your life.

- He was only a baby; you didn't get that attached to him.

- Your mother was pretty old, did you think she would live forever?

- He/she was only your friend.

- You can't stay sad forever.

- He/she had a good life.

- He/she wouldn't want you to be sad.

Four Easy Tips to Remember

1. Listen to the bereaved.

2. Be understanding.

3. You don't need to say very much.

4. JUST BE THERE FOR THEM.

How to Help Before the Funeral

OFFER TO NOTIFY THE SURVIVOR'S FAMILY AND FRIENDS ABOUT FUNERAL ARRANGEMENTS.

- Answer the phone and greet visitors.
- Keep a record of everyone who calls, visits or has been contacted.
- Help coordinate the food and beverage supply for the family and visitors, supplying food if necessary. In addition, coordinate paper goods, toilet paper, paper plates, utensils, and coffee should the family be receiving friends and loved ones into their home.
- Offer to pick up friends and family at the airport.
- Arrange housing or referrals to appropriate, nearby hotels or motels.
- Offer to provide transportation for out-of-town visitors.
- Help keep the house clean, and the dishes washed.
- House sit to prevent burglaries during the funeral and visitations.

Visitation or Viewing

Your presence at the visitation demonstrates that although someone has died, friends still remain. Your presence is an expression that you care.

Visitation provides a time and place for friends to offer their expression of sorrow and sympathy, rather than awkward strained conversation at the office, super-market or social activities.

The obituary will designate the hours of visitation when the family will be present and will designate the times when special services such as lodge services or prayer services may be held.

Personal visits at the funeral home are fine anytime during the suggested hours of the day or evening to pay respects, even though the family may not be present. Friends and relatives are requested to sign the register book, one's full name should be listed.

Friends should use their own judgment on how long they should remain at the funeral home or place of visitation. If one's presence is needed, one should offer to stay.

Helping After the Funeral

Consider doing these things every week for two or three months.

- Prepare or provide dinner on a day that is mutually acceptable.

- Offer to help with yard chores such as mowing, watering or pruning.

- Feed and exercise the pets.

- Write notes offering encouragement and support.

- Offer to drive or accompany the survivor to the cemetery regularly.

- Offer to house sit, so the survivor can take a restful vacation, or visit family or friends out of town.

- Make a weekly run to the grocery store, laundry or cleaners.

- Help with the thank uou notes and other correspondence.

- Anticipate difficult periods such as anniversaries, birthdays, holidays, and the day of the death.

- Always mention the decedent by name and encourage reminiscing.

Responding To Grief

Remember as a person works through the stages of their grief, "triggers" occur which can cause a renewal in the intensity of grief throughout the individual's lifetime.

Triggers may be as simple as a date on the calendar, hearing a certain song, observing children at play, watching a movie, the scent of a certain food, or receiving an invitation to a party or event in the mail.

Best practices to help a friend or relative recover

from grief.

1. Let the person talk about what has happened.

2. Learn what the loss means for them.

3. Be a good listener.

4. Ask open-ended questions.

5. Reflect their words back to them.

6. Try to understand if the loss is an isolated single event or part of a chain of losses.

7. Understand that this loss creates other losses. For example, a widow has not only lost her husband, she has lost her handyman, her confidant, and perhaps her financial advisor. The loss of her husband affects every aspect of her existence. She may not be prepared or capable of taking on these responsibilities herself.

8. Allow time for healing and adjustment to their new life without the deceased.

9. Try to identify and label feelings that are there. If they feel anger, labeling it and discussing it will help them overcome it with less confusion.

10. Suggest and explore creative ways to adjust to the feelings and reactions of this loss. Internalizing feelings allows the bereaved to develop coping methods that may not move them towards resolution.

11. Understand that exploration of "the new self" is rather like living through adolescence all over again. The bereaved must rediscover who they are without the benefit of the decedent in their life. This can be a difficult process. The bereaved might need socialization techniques and opportunities.

12. Explore available resources, people, organizations and activities, and identify their location. If you feel a support group might benefit your friend, find one that meets conveniently close to his/her home. You might also volunteer to attend the meetings with your friend. Doing so will help him/her enter back into a group setting without feeling overwhelmed.

13. Support those who are in turn acting in a supportive role for your friend. Reinforcing the concepts and practices suggested by the group leader will encourage your friend to accomplish the tasks.

14. Remember the need for practical support to assist day to day living. Bereft individuals may seem less organized or energetic as they have been in the past. They might need temporary assistance with basic tasks of daily living. Trips to the grocery store, laundry or yard chores are examples of tasks when your friend might need assistance.

15. Encourage all people affected by loss to interact when they are ready and able to do so. We all grieve and recover at our own pace. We should help our friends to recover in a way that is comfortable and practical for them.

16. During bereavement and extreme stress, communication skills may suffer. Communicate with the bereft at a level they can understand. Explain issues and instructions carefully. Never

assume understanding.

17. Explore the personal strengths and abilities of the bereft. Identify and label these resources for your friend. This helps your friend realize that they have value and that they can restructure their lives to function within their capacity once again.

18. Try to avoid using clichés and neat solutions. Most often, these offend rather than help.

19. Don't ever abuse trust or confidentiality. If your friend has said something in confidence that needs to be brought to the attention of someone else, discuss it with your friend first. Explain your reason for wanting to share their words.

20. Be prepared to take risks acknowledging the possible consequences. Sometimes we are uncomfortable with growth. Be sure your friend understands that you are there to help them recover and that you have recognized an area where they are stronger than they realize. Demonstrate the advantages to them for their growth risks and offer assistance in its accomplishment.

21. Be sensitive to possible "triggers" and special occasions that will arise and if appropriate, be there for those moments or events. Birthdays, anniversaries and holidays are often strong triggers and can result in emotional difficulties. Help your friend prepare when these dates are in the near future and be there with them if you can.

22. Be there, but give space.

23. Carefully identify defenses and coping styles that do not

promote constructive healing. Present opportunities and encourage exploration to develop better methods and skills when possible.

If you find that your help does not encourage positive results, back up and give your friend or loved one some breathing room. Reassure them that if they need your assistance, you are willing to help them to the degree they desire or need.

PART B

THE BUSINESS SIDE OF FUNERAL PLANNING

NO ONE FEELS LIKE FUNERAL PLANNING UPON THE DEATH OF A LOVED ONE. THIS SECTION OF PUSHIN' UP DAISIES WILL HELP YOU UNDERSTAND THE PROCESS. IT CONTAINS VALUABLE TIPS FOR THOSE IN AN AT-NEED SITUATION.

CHAPTER 7

PRE-NEED
BENEFITS AND FUNDING

The Benefits of Pre-Funding

Save Money

Like everything else in life, the cost of funerals continues to rise. When you pre-arrange a funeral, you guarantee tomorrow's services at today's prices. This process potentially saves you thousands of dollars, depending on the span of time between Pre-arrangement and death.

Pre-arrangements may also help you qualify for medical funding assistance while protecting your estate from governmental confiscation. Funds that have been legally attached to funeral expenses are off limits to the government.

Ease Your Family's Burden

Pre-arranging one's funeral saves your family from having to make important decisions about what you would have wanted. This little act of consideration on your part could save family relations for generations to come.

Children, parents, spouses, ex-step great uncles and others, have and will continue to second-guess the poor soul burdened with making the at-need arrangements. This moment in time is so taxing, has the potential to rip families apart, can be calamitously expensive and yet, is so easily avoidable...by you. Please do yourself, your family, your friends and your estate a huge favor; pre-arrange your funeral and save the poor soul, who would otherwise be taxed with it, the nightmare of making these difficult decisions at the worst time possible, upon your death.

Ensure That Your Wishes are Followed

Prearranging allows you to choose what will happen at your funeral. It ensures that everyone knows what you wanted to transpire and saves your loved ones the agony of trying to figure out what you would have wanted, had you taken care of this before your death.

If you have gone the extra mile and pre-funded your choices into a contract, you have ensured that undue burdens and unnecessary expenses are not placed upon the financial and emotional stability of your family.

When making selections and choices, consider and be mindful of their effects on your survivors. Remember funerals are for the living. Your survivors will be the ones who will suffer unfinished business, insurmountable debt and inconceivable loneliness. They will be adrift without your guiding influences, experience and love. Consider wisely the benefits of providing them with one last opportunity to experience a final farewell, mend their broken hearts or psychologically set right any unresolved issues.

Your decisions and actions regarding your last moments above ground, whether thoughtful or thoughtless, may facilitate your family on a journey from which they may reasonably recover, or one that will send them into the pitfalls of complicated grief.

Every effort possible should be invested to insure peace and resolution for all those who love you. Prepare them for this sorrowful day. Provide every opportunity possible, prior to death, for your loved one to say their final farewells. Openly and fervently express your loved, confidence and pride for them. Aloww them to clear any unresolved issues from their minds and accept responsibility for any wrong you may have ever inflicted upon them, whether purposely or not. These actions on your part will move them into a better recovery process and will provide you with equal peace as you close your history on earth.

A WORD OF CAUTION

Unfortunately, some funeral directors will act as if you are pre-arranging with them, when in fact you are not. If you do not have a written, signed and funded contract with all of the details included, you have no pre-arrangement at all. You have merely shopped the funeral home with no benefit to yourself whatsoever; an utter and complete waste of time and effort.

If you do have a contract, double-check it. Many times you will be shown details and will have made selections, which are not included in the total price of your contract. If this is the case, point it out to your funeral director or insurance agent and insist that these things be added into the contract.

One more noteworthy element of a pre-need funeral contract. Although most of the items in your pre-need funeral contract are frozen in price, many are not. Insist on knowing which items are guaranteed and which items are not. The items that are not guaranteed are those that are purchased or provided through a third party. The funeral home cannot guarantee another company's prices, therefore one should consider these items as estimates and understand that when the time comes, there may be a price increase on those items.

Decisions To Make

Vital Information

The decisions you make at this pre-arrangement conference are very important. You will decide whether to engage in a conventional funeral service or arrange for something tailored specifically toward your personality.

You will decide how much money is to be spent. You will decide whether to use burial or cremation services.

You can write your obituary, pick your music, design your programs, pick you own register book, make your memory movie, pick out your casket or urn, decide on a vault, select catering options, order keepsakes and the list goes on. All of these decisions will save your family much turmoil and money in the end. So, although it may seem daunting, carry on. Doing so is in your and your family's best interests.

Another very important part of the arrangement conference is the collection of vital information. Would you be surprised that most spouses don't know their mother-in-law's maiden name, or their spouse's social security number? There are so many facts that have to be gathered, and when a death occurs, one's memory and ability to think clearly are greatly impaired.

The following is a list of information one should bring when going to an arrangement conference. Consider writing this information in the spaces provided. In so doing, everything will be readily available when your family needs it.

Vital Statistics

Decedent's Name ______________________________

Decedent's Current address _________________________

Decedent's Sex ______________________________

Decedent's Ethnicity ______________________________

Decedent's Citizenship _____________________________

Decedent's Place of birth (including county) _____________

____

Decedent's Father's name _________________________

Decedent's Mother's name (maiden) _____________

Decedent's Marital status at time of death _____________

Name of Decedent's spouse (maiden) _____________

Decedent's Social security number ___________________

Decedent's Highest level of completed education _______

Decedent's Employment history ___________________

Decedent's Military service (dd214) ___________________

Decedent's Branch of service ______________________

Service dates ______________________

Service number ______________________

Obituary information

Decedent's Deceased relatives ____________

____

____

____

____

____

Decedent's Living relatives, their spouse's names and places of residence

Names of children ______________________

____

____

____

____

____

Brothers ______________________

____

____

____

____

Sisters ______________________

____

____

____

____

Grandchildren #________________________

Living History

A living history contains facts about your entire life, including clubs and fraternities in which you may have membership, hobbies, interests, community service, religious affiliation, special friends, pet's names, personality characteristics, special experiences, etc. An immense amount of information may be discussed and gathered at this conference.

Some things most people might not even know or remember about you, but they are still important and should be recorded.

Remember, the obituary is accepted as a genealogical document. It may be used to prove family lines of relation, insurance document verification, and many other very important things.

If in doubt, opt to write an obituary and publish it in the newspaper. Family members may someday be very grateful to you for your consideration in this matter.

A picture, as well, is a very important aspect of your history. Consider including two pictures, one of your younger self and one close to the age of your death. Friends and descendants alike will greatly appreciate this thoughtful element in your obituary. A third picture is appropriate if it highlights a specific accomplishment or award in your life's history.

A PERSONAL TESTIMONY OF OBITUARIES

I recently had a case where a young widow's husband had purchased a side policy of life insurance of which she was unaware. The sole piece of evidence hinging payment of this well-sized sum of funds was the evidence of a printed obituary in a dated newspaper.

If she had forgone the obituary, as some do, she might have lost this very generous endowment left to her, out of the consideration of her loving husband. By the way, this endowment saved this young widow's home and kept a roof over the heads of her young children.

Think twice before you forgo your obituary.

PRE-NEED VS. PRE-ARRANGEMENT

There is a difference between Pre-Arrangements and a funded Pre-Need Funeral Contract, both industry terms. Although it may seem obvious when reading these pages, I see many people who have fallen prey to this unfortunate misunderstanding.

A Pre-Arrangement is not the same as a Pre-Need Funeral Contract. A Pre-Arrangement is just that, an arrangement. There is no signed contract. You have made selections of funeral goods and services, but you have not contracted nor funded your choices. Even if you have received a contract looking paper with your choices recorded on it, unless you have paid for these choices, they are not yours.

It is similar to going to the mall and choosing a beautiful dress for prom. The very first one you try on fits perfectly. You absolutely love it, but because it is the first one you have tried, you ask the salesperson to put it on hold. You can't pick the very first one you try on, so you go to a few other shops and try on a few other dresses. You also ask her to write the price down along with the tax on the hold ticket, so that you know exactly how much this beautiful dress is going to cost. After shopping a few other stores, you convinced that the dress you put on hold at the first shop, is the perfect on for you. Now you need to go back and get the dress. When you hand the hold ticket to the salesperson, she will retrieve the dress for you and ring it up on her register. You must now make payment for the dress. Merely placing it on hold does not make it yours. The dress remains the property of the shop owner until you pay for it. One other note, if you have waited too long to come back for the dress, you may find that it no longer is available or that the price has increased. The same holds true for funeral products.

A Pre-Need Funeral Contract (referred to as a Pre-Need) is a signed and funded contract of funeral goods and services. In lay terms, this means that you have visited a funeral home; you have made choices on services and goods to be consumed in the accomplishment of your final wishes; you have recorded these choices into a contract, and you have provided funding for these choices.

A contract provides consideration for both parties listed in the agreement. You will receive the goods and services chosen, and the funeral provider will receive your money.

Those are the facts. Without them, there is no contract, and there is no Pre-Need. If you have only made Pre-Arrangements, your choices and selections are not guaranteed, your prices are not guaranteed, and your family will have to go through this wretched process once you die, along with funding it at potentially higher prices.

You may think that this is harsh, or perhaps an unnecessary explanation of this term. I assure you, this is not the case.

Daily I witness families that think they have a Pre-Need because they went into a funeral home and chose goods and services for a loved one's funeral prior to death.

Unfortunately, when they sit down, and I ask them for their Pre-Need Contract, I am sadly the bearer of bad news. They did not enter into a contract with the funeral home they visited. They only made choices. They did not back it up with a legal, signed contract. They did not make payment for the choices they made.

Quite often, they may even have a piece of paper that greatly resembles a contract. This paper may even list the various selections in the appropriate spaces. It is important to understand however, that this is merely a fancy list designed to suggest that you have agreed and committed yourself to this particular funeral home, when in fact, you have not. This piece of paper means nothing unless a pre-need funeral contract was signed and funded at the same time.

If the family has not pre-paid for these items by means of a pre-need funeral contract, they are not entitled to any of their selections nor do they have any guaranteed pricing. They are now subject to current prices and increases, and need to provide the necessary funds immediately upon necessity.

Another sad scenario that seems rather common is that a family may have entered a funeral home, made various selections and entered into a pre-need funeral contract. The common issue is that, although the family selected a complete funeral, only some of the items selected are listed in the pre-need funeral contract. Therefore, the family is confused thinking they are paying for a complete funeral, when in reality, they have only paid for some of their selections. The other items must now be paid for at current market prices.

One might wonder why or how could this possibly happen? The harsh truth of this scenario is the funeral home may have thought this particular family would choose their funeral home only if the price was lower than others they may have already visited. In this case, although the family was shown everything they needed for the funeral of their choice, the funeral home only agreed to some of the services and merchandise in order to keep the total from being a deal breaker. They know that the family will come to their funeral home at the necessary time and in such a situation of sadness, confusion and stress, they will just write a check to cover the balance.

Consider the following: If the choices are unfunded, they are also unsecured. What this means to you is that if ten years ago you picked out a steel casket for $200.00, in today's market that same casket may be priced at $3,600.00. Now you have an issue. You thought you had secured that casket for $200.00, but you didn't. Now you must come up with $3,600.00, perhaps more, in the next few minutes. This can create a substantial financial burden and exacerbate emotional stress, neither of which you would want your loved ones to experience at this difficult time.

MY PROFESSIONAL ADVICE

If you have a Pre-Need, take it to a different funeral home and ask them to evaluate it for you. Let them explain what is included in your Pre-Need and what is lacking. Protect yourself from funeral funding woes. Just as you would with your health care, seek a second professional opinion. You never know, you may find that you are perfectly set-up with all of the necessary elements needed to carry out your final wishes, but if not, it is better to be safe than sorry.

In all honesty, there are few funeral homes that will purposefully deceive client families. Many funeral homes and funeral directors simply feel that they know best, and in order to your time or keep your stress at a lower level, they make decisions on your behalf without your consent. If the funeral home you have chosen is one of these funeral homes, wouldn't you rather know it now than find out later? In my opinion, it is better to find out what your funeral home is up to before you are in a crisis situation. The way to do this is simple. Just as you would seek out a second opinion when your doctor suggests surgery, seek it out with your funeral arrangements. Make an appointment with a funeral home in a neighboring city and ask them to review your arrangements with you. Let them know that you just want to make sure all of your bases are covered. Tell them what you think you have arranged and they will tell you if your understanding and your paperwork matches. My purpose here is to merely encourage you to protect yourself.

FUNDING PRODUCTS

There are many products available to pre-fund your funeral choices. There are trust-funded policies, insurance funded policies, annuities, and many other options.

There are endless insurance companies, and each company has unique and different products. My best advice is to be sure that when you buy a funeral policy, you check and double check, that all of the goods and services selected are included in its language. Also verify there is a payment start date and a payment end date.

At this point, it is important that you understand the vital differences between life insurance and pre-need funeral insurance. Although it is possible to pay for your funeral needs with life insurance, it is not your best option.

Life insurance is designed for life's expenses. It is a never ending bill, the premium increases over time while the benefit decreases or expires over time. It is not protected from Medicaid nor does it freeze funeral prices.

Pre-need insurance has a beginning payment and an ending payment. Premiums do not increase and once paid in full, the benefits remain on account until you need them. Your funds also increase with interest. Funeral prices are frozen due to the interest gained.

All too often, I see clients that have a policy they have been paying on for over 45 years. Even though they have paid in five times what the policy will pay out, they cannot stop paying on it because if they do, they will lose all of the money they have paid up to that point. Another concern is the insured may now be in poor health or older than insurable age as accepted by the insurance company.

Don't be one of these people. Don't get taken advantage of for life.

If you find that you have one of these policies, and you have crossed a road in your life where you would no longer qualify for a sound insurance policy, you have a choice to make. You might choose to cancel this policy and start a new policy, hoping that you make it past the "we'll only pay out what you've paid in" clause (usually for the first two years from the commencement date). Alternatively, you have to continue paying on the rip-off policy until the day you die.

I had a sweet family come into my office with one of these policies. I evaluated the policy for them. Over the past 45 years, they had paid $47,000.00. This policy was written to cover both the husband and the wife. Now that they were no longer newlyweds and were facing aging illnesses, they wanted to bring their policy over to my funeral home and assign it to us for their future deaths.

We called the issuing insurance company, and asked for the payout value. The total sum of the payout was $5,000.00, not for each of them, but combined. They each had $2,500.00 in funds to cover their final expenses.

As if this were not bad enough, this sweet couple was locked into a policy where they could not stop paying each month, or it would cancel. Unfortunately, due to their age and illnesses, they would no longer qualify for a reasonable, affordable policy so they were stuck continuing with this terrible policy.

If you have one of these policies, seek the advice of your funeral practitioner. Fortunately, these policies are no longer legal to sell (at least in Texas, unless your particular insurance company is grandfathered in), but my advice remains as before,

"When purchasing a funeral contract, funded by insurance or any other means, seek a second opinion."

Of course, insurance policies always cost more than they pay out. You are paying for the possibility that you might die before you finish paying the policy, and for that service, the insurance company wants to be well paid. The point is, however, you should never pay over twice what the policy pays out. You certainly should never pay over eight times its value.

CHAPTER 8

AT NEED SOLUTIONS

WHAT IS AT-NEED

Funding a funeral when the deceased did not prepare in advance of death by purchasing a Pre-Need or life insurance policy is called "At-Need Funding."

At-Need Funding is sometimes difficult for the family, especially if death was unexpected or sudden. If steps were not taken in advance of death, the family might find themselves in an awkward situation where the necessary funds for all of their funeral needs may not be readily available.

In this situation, the family must pool their funds together to be able to cover the final expenses, or ask for outside help from their community or religious organization. Credit cards may also be drawn upon to procure the necessary funding.

If there is still a shortfall after taking these steps to gather the necessary funds for the funeral expenses, members of the family might offer real property as collateral for the lending of funds. This is called a secured loan and is most often solicited through a banking or lending institution.

If you find yourself in this predicament, there are certain pearls of knowledge that will help you save money. Moreover, even though it may seem outrageously expensive, and others might wonder if it is worth it, (you might even wonder this yourself,) there is long term and far reaching value in a traditional funeral experience.

I will list a few facts to help you find ways to save on the expenses, however, if you have not prepared emotionally or spiritually for such an experience, you might search out a practitioner in these areas.

You have to be willing to be strong at a time when all your strength is focused on just functioning. It is a difficult time, however if you will keep these few things in mind, you will be better able to deal with the circumstances, than if you were going in blind.

First, if you have not prepared for a funeral in advance, you need to be prepared for the expense of it. During this experience, you are going to be angry with the funeral home, irritated with your funeral director, aggravated at family members and possibly resentful toward the decedent.

Just as life is not a trivial matter, neither is death.

Often near the end of life, if one has not prepared financially for death, we hear them say, "What does it matter, I'm already gone, just put me in a box and throw me in the ground", or words to that effect.

Although it is true that one is already gone, the fact remains that one's loved ones are not. Moreover, the passing of one's presence from among them is difficult for them to bear.

It would behoove you, and those around you, to realize in advance that the loss of a beloved family member or friend is not a lighthearted matter, nor is it easy to bear.

Be prepared for a difficult experience that will last for weeks, months, possibly even years.

One should do all that is possible in advance of death, making it easier for those left behind to grieve and recover from ones loss.

Diminish their suffering before it begins by taking responsibility for your funeral choices and expenses, and allow them to concentrate on surviving the hardest day they will ever experience. Doing this will be one of the kindest things you have ever done for your survivors.

Nevertheless, this section is for families that have not had the advantage of pre-planning, so let's see what we can do to help them through this experience.

Number One

The number one thing to realize is that you have the power to say "No."

"No, that does not suit my budget."

"No, that does not satisfy my need."

"No, I do not need anything extra."

Memorize these three statements and you will come out of the arrangement conference, even though you may not realize it, with a more reasonable funeral expense.

Number Two

The second most important thing for you to know is that you do not have to buy everything your funeral director presents to you even though she assumes you will.

At certain funeral homes, there is a required amount of dollars each funeral must meet. As a funeral director I have been at funeral homes where the funeral must not sell for less than $14,000.00, while at other funeral homes, they only need to sell for $4,000.00. This is important to know if you are faced with a death that was not expected or pre-funded.

You can certainly understand that if a funeral director is required to sell you $14,000.00 worth of funeral goods and services, he is going to suggest that you add a lot of things to your bill that might be unnecessary. Moreover, things may be priced a bit higher at this funeral home than at another one.

Remember, you are a consumer.

My mother had a "Golden Rule" for consuming.

"My momma told me, You better shop around."

You are consuming funeral services and funeral goods for the death of your loved one. When you buy a new car, what do you do? You visit different car lots, check the classifieds, check out eBay. What about a new prom dress? You go to the mall and look in five or six shops. You go to a bridal store or two until you find one that you like and can afford.

The same concept is true when you are in need of a funeral. Unfortunately, in the case of a funeral, time is short. Moreover, shopping funeral homes is the last thing on your list of fun things you want to do. The reality is, however, if funds are an issue, shopping around can be very financially advantageous.

Do not be shy or intimidated.

Ask why you need certain things. Are they required by law? Make sure your funeral director can satisfy your questions with a legitimate need.

Perhaps the cemetery you have chosen requires a casket and a cement vault for burial.

Vaults are not required by law, only be certain cemeteries.

Therefore, simply choosing a different cemetery could save potentially thousands of dollars.

Your funeral director knows all of these little things and can help you make more affordable choices if you will just ask, or insist, depending on your funeral home's business practices. If at this point, your funeral director is persistent in adding high dollar and insignificant expenses to your services, change funeral directors, better yet, change funeral homes.

Perhaps you do not know what some of the things are that have been placed on your list of funeral goods and services. If you are unsure about something, ask about it.

Remember, your funeral director has a college education in funeral service. After graduation from college and completion of interning, many funeral directors remain confused with funeral pricing. If they have trouble after all of that, don't you think they would be patient in helping you to understand it too?

No one expects you to understand what is or is not necessary when it comes to funeral goods and services. Ask your funeral director if there is anything on your contract that could be eliminated. Ask for alternative services? Ask them if they have ever been in your situation and what they did to make it better? If they haven't been in your situation, I can almost guarantee you that they have helped someone in your situation and they know ways to lower your costs. Just ask.

A good funeral director will protect your interests and guide you through this process. If this is not the case, you are most likely at a high numbers funeral home and you should probably consider moving your loved one to a more reasonably priced and perhaps a more ethical funeral home.

As a new funeral director, I would study the General Price List over and over, asking more experienced directors what all of those little things listed were. It can be confusing.

Do not be afraid to ask for information or clarification.

If you find that your funeral director is not forthcoming, cooperative or helpful, perhaps you are at the wrong funeral home.

My advice would be to get up and go to a different funeral home, one that is more forthcoming, cooperative and helpful. Do not be afraid to get up and leave. Just because you walked into a funeral home and asked a few questions, does not obligate you to hold your funeral there.

How shocking is that? You might be wondering, "How can I get up and leave, if they have my daddy in the back room somewhere?" Well, it is quite simple, just get up and leave.

They can not do anything with your daddy until you give them permission to do so. And here's a news flash for you. Do not let them intimidate you, they are not going to do anything to your daddy before they have the money to pay for whatever needs to be done. (Well, other than embalming. Due to the time sensitivity associated with embalming, all they require to proceed is your permission.)

If you have given your permission for embalming, payment for these services will be required before you can move your dad somewhere else. If you leave and go to another funeral home, the second funeral home may only charge you for the services and goods you use from them. And guess what, the first funeral home can only do the same.

So you see, you are not going to be billed for the same thing twice, but leaving one funeral home and going to another puts both funeral homes on notice that they should not trifle with you. You may find that both funeral homes seem a little more cooperative at this point.

The second funeral home will call the first funeral home and ask them for their charges; they will add these charges to your bill, and they will then pay the first funeral home on your behalf. Your daddy will then be transferred to the second funeral home, and you can proceed with your funeral experience.

So now that we have learned how not to be a passive funeral consumer, what else do we need to know?

Number Three

The third most important thing to know about At-Need arrangements is how the money works for the funeral home in an At-Need situation verses a Pre-Need situation.

A Pre-Need funding situation is based on hedging. Your funeral home has a mark-up factored into their price points based on averages: an average of profit versus an average on expense; an average based on habits of people realizing their mortality; and many other factors.

They are also hedging the interest rates on the policies, hoping to grow your money enough to cover your final expenses and still be in a profitable situation.

Now, if your purchase is At-Need and their prices are based on Pre-Need hedging, how might you use this to your advantage?

The answer is very simple; ask for a reduction.

If the casket is priced at $1,000.00 because they are predicting that steel over a 10-year Pre-Need might double, there is quite possibly plenty of wiggle room in the price for an at-need situation. Do not be afraid to ask for a discount.

There are a multitude of expenses in your funeral services that are not monies that go to the funeral home, and in such a case, the funeral director would not be able to discount those services or goods.

For instance, you might think that the charge for the open and close is too high. An open and close is a service provided by a dirt service company. They have heavy equipment and operators that dig the grave and close it back up, once the committal services are completed. They also provide a tent and chairs at the gravesite. This service is outsourced by the funeral home and is, therefore, a cash advance service. If you ask your funeral director to discount it, he might tell you that he cannot because it is a cash advance service.

CASH ADVANCE services and items are items or services the funeral director or funeral home offers to compliment your service on behalf of someone else or some other company. Your funeral director would be unable to adjust those prices without conferring with that entity. If your funeral director tells you this, don't be afraid to ask him to either adjust your cost somewhere else or to call this other business and ask them for a reduction on your behalf. After all, all they can say is no, and if so, you still have the option to go elsewhere or to accept the charges as listed. The fact is, it is your choice. Choose according to your needs.

Last Resort, At-Need Funding Solutions

At-Need funerals can be very difficult to finance, so be ready to ask family, friends, community, clergy, acquaintances, long lost cousins, neighbors and benevolent souls to help.

You may want to put it in the obituary…

"In lieu of flowers, our family asks that donations be made on daddy's behalf to the funeral home to help cover the unexpected expenses of his sudden death."

You may not want to announce it to the world by newspaper, so you could choose another option.

You might ask your family and friends individually and privately to help.

You may want to ask your clergy to take up a special offering to apply toward your expenses at church next week.

You may want to ask your dad's special club or fraternity to host a fundraiser in his honor.

The point is there are infinite means to find funds to help pay for an unexpected funeral. And, people who love the deceased are willing to help when they can.

In cases of sudden or unexpected death, there should be no shame. Death is unpredictable; we never know when it might suddenly be upon us. As living beings, we do not seek death. We therefore avoid its consideration until we are elderly or gravely ill.

Friends and family grieve the loss of your loved one, and helping to cover these expenses will help them feel like they did something for their deceased friend or family member when he or she could not do it himself or herself.

Helping when needed, will also help friends and family recover from the grief of the loss. They will have a feeling of peace, usefulness and fulfillment. These feeling aid them to experience less complicated grief and assists easier recovery.

SUPER SAVER TIP

It is known that walking into the casket room to pick out a casket in an At-Need case is simply too overwhelming. Because it is so difficult and stressful, most families will choose a casket from the first five nearest the door. Of course, the first five nearest the door are strategically placed to be higher priced caskets. To save money on your casket selection, shield your eyes and walk into the middle of the room. The caskets in the middle of the room are more moderately priced.

If these caskets are still priced higher than you would like to pay, don't forget to ask about the "roll in model." The roll-in model is generally less desirable and inferior in a multitude of ways with function and appearance being the most obvious. If money is an issue, however, take a look at it and you may find that it is just what the budget needs.

DOWNGRADE SERVICES

If after all of these tactics have not successfully brought your funeral expenses down to an affordable level, you might consider downgrading your services.

Rather than a complete traditional funeral, you might consider a graveside service. If a graveside service is still too expensive, consider an immediate burial or a direct cremation.

CHAPTER 9

THE GENERAL PRICE LIST
GPL

The General Price List, GPL

Funeral pricing is a difficult concept to understand. The primary reason for the difficulty is that federal bureaucracy is in control of most of the language one must incorporate into the General Price List.

Even the name "General Price List" is controlled by the government. If the funeral home wanted to title its price list "My Funeral Home's Price List" it would be in violation of federal regulations. Perhaps to accommodate its internet site, the funeral home would like to use the term "Website Price List" or "Menu." Again, it would be in violation of federal regulations and in danger of steep fines and possible loss of licensure.

The second reason the GPL can be difficult to understand is that the funeral industry has not really changed its way of doing business since the civil war. Have you read a newspaper or any written word from that era? If you have, you realize that things have changed, that is, except for the funeral industry's way of doing business. Your great grandmother might have an easier time making sense of the "General Price List" than you.

With all of that aside, let us see if we can shed some light on understanding the "General Price List" and the theory of funeral pricing.

Before I entered the funeral business, I was a successful artist. I worked with my husband in our national photography business, Angel Shots, Inc. Our extensive experience in the retail market has somewhat jaded our outlook on the antiquity of funeral service, and its pricing practices. If you ask a Funeral Arts College Professor, he most likely will have no idea on the science surrounding:

A. Price Points: the retail PRICE of a product, determined in such a way as to compete with PRICES of other products.

B. Market Share: the percentage of an industry or market's total sales that is earned by a particular company over a specified time period.

C. Merchandising: Any practice that contributes to the sale of products to a retail consumer.

Funeral Arts College Professors are generally older gentlemen with an extensive history in funeral service, or they are merely academics set up to teach a subject in which they have little to no experience or understanding. They are merely passing along information that has remained the same for centuries.

Traditionally, a funeral home is passed through a certain "Funeral Family" for generation upon generation. These "Funeral Families" have been doing business the same way ever since their great-great grandfather started their business, and the easiest way of doing things is through the path of least resistance, so they keep on keeping on, as they always have.

Imagine this: as the owner of a state-of-the-art digital photography company managing portrait studios nationwide, a digital artist, graphics design artist and a digital touchup artist, I was very familiar with card readers; a device that translates the information from your camera card into readable format for your computer. Then one day, while sitting in what is generally considered one of the top funeral colleges in America, I was quite surprised. My college professor was speaking of a card reader that read what was commonly referred to as "punch cards" from the 1950's and early 1960's, as if it were today's modern method of an office information system.

When I realized what he was teaching, I questioned him about it. He informed me that this was the information that would be on the national conference board exams.

So yes, even the governmental agencies involved in funeral service still remain as antiquated as most of the funeral industries funeral homes.

When you go to a funeral home to make funeral arrangements, and you find that you are completely confused, realize that they are functioning in a different century than the one in which you live. It will make things less frustrating even though they will remain confusing.

Often a point of confusion, and even though I've stated this previously, please indulge me as I re-visit the difference between Pre-Need and At-Need funeral arrangements. It is vitally important that you understand the distinction and why they are handled differently. You will be much better prepared if you are fluent in these structural concepts.

In funeral service, there are two different types of funeral pricing. There are At-Need funerals, and there are Pre-Need funerals.

An At-Need funeral is a funeral that is arranged and paid for at the time of death.

A Pre-Need funeral is one that is planned and paid for in advance of death.

The reason this concerns you is the cost.

Although pre-need funerals are higher priced, they offer you the opportunity to pay for your funeral choices on a payment schedule while freezing the prices for your selected goods and services. In order to ensure that the funeral home is able to guarantee these prices over the course of your life, a buffer is built into the price. This buffer is called hedging and it is coupled with the interest accrued on your policy funds. Through these two concepts, the funeral home hopes to make a profit on your funeral while offering you the opportunity and convenience to pay for it over time.

If one goes to a funeral home to arrange a Pre-Need funeral, he or she will select merchandise and services from the "General Price List." He or she will also arrange a suitable method to pre-pay for his or her choices. This is considered good planning as it freezes tomorrow's funeral at today's prices.

At this juncture, one might ask, "How does that work?" If one buys something today but does not take delivery of it for ten years, how does the funeral home not lose money through inflation? A very good question. The answer is through hedging and interest.

The prices on the pre-need "General Price List" (GPL) have an average of inflation built into them. The funeral home is going to mark up their goods and services based on what history has proven as an average inflation rate over a certain period. Well, at least reputable funeral homes will do so.

The second half of the inflation equation, the one that protects the funeral home, is the interest on your pre-paid funeral funds (through the insurance company). The insurance company is going to invest your money and attach a certain percentage of interest to it as long as it remains in their coffers. When you die, your funeral home will claim the policy value and any interest accrued over the life of the policy. The interest and the inflation average built into the price point is the hedging that the funeral home counts on to remain viable.

This works out to be a good system for the consumer and the funeral home as long as the economy moves along in an upward swing. This plan allows the consumer to pay for his or her funeral expense over time at an outdated price, and it allows the funeral home to hedge so that when you die, it does not lose money on the contract.

If your funeral home does not offer lower At-Need pricing, then they are taking advantage of you. They may even be charging you more in the present to help cover any flaws in their hedging of funeral costs of the past. You may indeed be paying for their pricing mistakes on Pre-Needs maturing in today's markets.

Some funeral homes may not list lower pricing for At-Need clients, because it confuses to the client and they don't want to explain why a Pre-Need person has to pay more for the same product. Although is it a sound and legal practice, it is very confusing to the consumer and it erodes confidence in the funeral home.

The reason for this practice is simple if you have a degree in economics and understand inflation and interest offsets. Few of us however, have this understanding, and so the equation remains confusing. Simply stated, the Pre-Need client is not taking delivery of the product they are purchasing. This delay is subject to increases in manufacturing and raw materials. Prices will adjust to allow for inflation over this delay. Thus to compensate for this increase, the funeral establishment must price hedge to overcome historical inflationary indexing.

Not so easy to understand, not so easy to swallow.

The practice of two price sheets, one for At-Need and another for Pre-Need is an accepted practice, designed to bypass confusing the consumer. This system is a fair system. The funeral home and insurance company are the entities taking the risk.

I have advised many clients in other states and other areas about at-need pricing and it seems that several funeral homes insist that there is no such thing. So that you may understand that there definitely are two different pricing structures, I list here a direct quote from the Federal Trade Commission's Complying with the Funeral Rule, June 2004. **"Because you may sell different goods and services on a pre-need basis, your pre-need GPL may vary from the GPL you use in at-need situations."** (FTC June 2004, Complying with the Funeral Rule, page 5)

Your options are to pre-plan, purchasing your funeral goods and services in advance, so that you can make affordable payments on your choices, or forgo pre-planning and gamble that when the time comes, you might be able to afford the hyper inflated price of your funeral expenses.

In this circumstance, you have decided to take the risk of inflation upon yourself, rather than allowing the funeral home and insurance company to do so. The choice is yours. If you decide to take the risk upon yourself, realize that inflation can be a nasty and extremely costly business.

Herein lies the question, why is the consumer being shown pre-need prices if they are in an at-need situation? Unfortunately, most funeral homes do not share this pricing science with their funeral directors. If a funeral director does not understand this pricing structure, or is unaware of any price differences for the at-need client, they are unable to pass it on to their clients. Over time and through the various levels of funeral home management, the knowledge of this two tier pricing structure has been lost. In its effort to eradicate deceptive practices, the FTC has created so much confusion that the educated and experienced funeral personnel are completely unable to understand this concept. In such a situation, the pricing structures seem even more deceptive and therefore, most funeral homes have chosen to just ignore the opportunity to offer lower prices in at-need situations. Unfortunately, this has resulted in at-need clients paying pre-need prices for their funeral goods and services. This concept has had the absolute opposite effect on its intended outcome.

So, what to do for At-Need situations with Pre-Need prices? There are a number of remedies available. First, realize that it exists and be prepared to defend it. The funeral home may offer packages with an At-Need discount available. However, as I stated before, most funeral homes do not like to offer two different prices for what the consumer perceives as the same product.

The funeral home does not want to put this information out there because it confuses and angers their Pre-Need clients. It is just easier to assume that everyone takes advantage of Pre-Needs and not worry about it any longer.

Unfortunately, At-Need consumers suffer from this if the funeral home does not educate their funeral directors in the science of funeral hedging. In my experience, this is, unfortunately, the case at approximately 98% of funeral homes. I, myself only show the different prices on my price list on two products. Of course, if my clients are At-Need; I offer a discount off of the total, once all of the selections are finalized. The discount I offer is my current cost without the Pre-Need hedging factored into the price point.

Your chosen funeral home may offer your final total to you in this non-specific discounted manner. If their pricing is based on a 50% mark-up with an added 25% inflation allowance for Pre-Need contracts, the funeral home may say to you, "Your At-Need choices have totaled $5,000.00, the funeral home is prepared to discount your total to $3,750.00." There may not seem to be any obvious reason for this discount they have offered, but if you understand the difference between At-Need and Pre-Need price points, you will instantly understand why they have offered you this discount. Hypothetically of course, a 25% inflation allowance is rather unrealistic. You are probably looking at somewhere more in the 3% to 5% inflation discount allowance.

The point is, however, if the discount is not forthcoming, you might look at switching to a different funeral home.

Do not be afraid to ask your funeral director about these price points. He may not even understand the pricing himself, and often he is expected to sell his funerals at a dollar average well above what the consumer is comfortable with paying, but be fearless. Push forward and ask. It can't hurt. Any discount is better than no discount. If they refuse an At-Need discount, ask them to explain the reason. If it makes sense to you, then everything is fine. If not, go to a different funeral home.

Even if your loved one is in the custody of this funeral home and you decide you are not happy with them, you can have your loved one transferred to a different funeral home of your choice. It is not difficult, and it is illegal for the first funeral home to be uncooperative in releasing the deceased as per your wishes. Do not be afraid to be assertive.

A few more things about pricing and then we will move on. There is only one item on the GPL that you must agree to pay. It is listed as non-declinable (an FTC term). The non-declinable item on the GPL is the charge for Basic services of Funeral Director and Staff. Everything else is declinable.

You must realize however, when certain choices are made, other companion expenses will follow. For instance, embalming is not required except in certain circumstances. What does that mean? If you have suffered a death in your family and you bury your loved one within 24 hours, you are not required to embalm him/her. If you would rather postpone burial for a few days and have a visitation and funeral service, then suddenly embalming becomes a requirement.

The Federal Trade Commission regulates funeral language, and it is, therefore, inherently confusing. It's just the way it is when the government controls your words.

My best advice is the same advice I offered before,

Seek a second opinion,

Ask for explanations,

and always without failure…

ask for any wiggle room on the final total...

"A discount."

To prepare financially and emotionally for the expense of a funeral, utilize the worksheets at the end of this book.

These worksheets include a sample General Price List (GPL) and teaches you how to read it. Once you understand all of the items on the GPL, you can utilize its work pages to help you select only the items you want for your funeral services.

CHAPTER 10

PRICING
FULL SERVICE OR PARTIAL SERVICE

Partial Services aka Penny Savers

To help you save money, your funeral home offers a few "Penny Saver" deals. These too are controlled by the FTC, both in language and content. Remember, to save money you must be willing to do without or do for yourself.

Penny Saver deals are considered "Partial Services" by the FTC. They are labeled "Partial Services" because they only contain a percentage of the usually accepted services associated with a traditional funeral or cremation service.

Deciding to pay for only part of the services associated with your service requires that you provide the other services or do without them. Usually this may cause you to be inconvenienced by having to do certain aspects of the service yourself. It may even be embarrassing, but if you don't want to pay your the funeral home to do these things, you are going to have to do them yourself.

It is very similar to purchasing an airplane ticket. We all want to fly first class and sit in the roomy seats while the flight attendant serves steak and wine, but in reality, most of us sit in the cheap seats with stranger's elbows poking our ribs, and have little or nothing to eat or drink.

The reality of air travel is that if you want the experience of first class, you must pay for it or suffer the discomfort and possible embarrassment of cheap seats. The same holds true in funeral service. If you want the first-class services offered by the funeral home, you must pay for them or suffer the discomfort and possible embarrassment of partial or cheap services.

Immediate Burial

An Immediate Burial is exactly as its name suggests...immediate. This service does not contain any traditional services. It is carried out within 24 hours of death, at the convenience of the funeral home without consideration to the family.

You may wonder what "without consideration to the family" means. It means that most likely, the family will not see their deceased loved one again after he/she leaves their custody. The funeral home will accept custody of your loved one at the place of death and will transport him/her to their funeral home. Your loved one will be placed in a burial box or casket, and buried within a 24-hour period. There will not be an embalming, no viewing, no visitation, no funeral service, not even a burial service for you to attend. The funeral home will bury the body at their convenience.

You will pay for the applicable share of the non-declinable professional services of the funeral director and staff, the first call, purchase of the casket or burial box. You will also pay for the open and close of the grave. Things you will not pay for are those that do not apply under this type of burial. Things for which you will not pay are the full professional services charge for the funeral director and staff, embalming, a visitation, a funeral service, programs, register book, hearse, and numerous other things.

The cost will vary according to the funeral home you choose, but I guarantee, it will cost less than a traditional funeral. You must remember though; you have forgone any services and you will not view your loved one nor in most cases, attend the burial process.

Direct Cremation

A Direct Cremation is exactly as its name suggests... direct. This service does not contain any traditional services. Once your loved one dies, you will call the funeral home, and they will collect the deceased. There are no services associated with this choice. Your loved one goes from place of death directly to the crematory. You will not see the deceased once the funeral home takes him/her away.

You will receive a phone call to come to the funeral home and collect the cremains of your loved one once the cremation is complete. The funeral home will not offer you any other services - no visitation, no viewing, no memorial service, no flower services, nothing.

I mention the lack of flower services because everyone wants to send flowers. Because you have decided to forego services, the funeral home will not receive any flowers for you.

You need to inform your family and friends where they should send the flowers. Be prepared as well for angry friends and relatives. I would estimate that at least 77% of the direct cremations I perform result in familial squabbles. Although others are not paying for any services, many of your friends and relatives will be insulted that you did not pay for services either. They expect you to pay and offer them the traditional services related to death. When these services are not available, feelings get hurt and tempers flare.

Remember, the funeral is not for the deceased, it is for the survivors. Many survivors find it very difficult to accept death without witnessing the deceased and having that one last opportunity to say good-bye.

If you feel that your friends and family may find direct cremation difficult to handle, you might consider cremation with a more traditional selection of services to accompany it. I will explain some of these options in the Traditional Choices section of this chapter.

Graveside Service

A graveside service is exactly as its name suggest...beside the grave. When one chooses a graveside service, they expect to forego many of the comforts and services associated with a traditional funeral service.

A graveside service is less expensive than a traditional funeral service because it provides less service. It utilizes less time in the funeral home and less time from the funeral home staff. That is the reason it costs less.

A graveside service is held at the place of interment. If you have chosen a local cemetery or mausoleum, the service will be conducted at that site. Visitations are not included within the graveside services list of events. As the graveside service is conducted at the location of interment, memory movies, programs, music, multiple participants, etc. are simply not necessary.

The graveside officiant will be quick with any words he/she might deliver out of consideration for the comfort and safety of those in attendance. Safety and dignity, of the decedent, are paramount concerns and subject to deterioration with prolonged exposure to the elements. There is generally only one person conducting the event. They will usually offer something brief in reflection of the life that has passed and offer a prayer for closure. Flowers, music, poems, eulogies, etc. are generally forgone and not included within the ceremony. The graveside committal service is usually limited in time by the funeral home in order to minimize expenses and afford you the savings you are seeking.

When one chooses a graveside service, they should consider that their friends, relatives, guests and the deceased shall be exposed to the elements for a brief period. Precautions should be taken to ensure that your guests are not exposed to prolonged periods of time to the hot sun, cold wind, rain, lightening, wildlife, etc.

A graveside service is lower in cost because it does not offer the use of a building or church, music, funeral home staff or equipment, visitations, receptions, memory items, etc.

The service is simple and quick.

TRADITIONAL CHOICES

Traditional Funeral Services are more expensive than Partial Funeral Services. They offer many more service options, and the funeral home and staff will be taking care of and performing all of those inconvenient details and duties of which you stand in need.

I can't even begin to list all of the things your funeral director does for you. The list is too long and varies from family to family. A good funeral director is worth every cent you are paying. A good funeral director takes care of all of the details and duties necessary to get your loved one legally buried with dignity and honor. A good funeral director takes these duties upon herself so that you can enter the mourning process and grieve with your family and friends.

Traditional Funeral choices and Traditional Cremation choices offer an endless range for customization. For instance, rather than foregoing the traditional services associated with death as with a direct cremation, you may elect to include a visitation with your cremation.

Including a visitation with your cremation allows your friends and family to view the deceased, witness that death has actually occurred, offer comfort and condolences to each other and verify that your body is actually the one being cremated.

Many families feel a void when they have been denied the opportunity to verify the decedent or give their last respects before cremation occurs. Quite possibly, a simple visitation could nullify complicated grief for family and friends in this situation.

Traditional service options are available when one is choosing cremation. Of course, cremation with traditional service options costs more than a direct cremation. If you choose to add traditional services to your cremation, the funeral home and funeral director are called upon to invest additional hours into your final disposition process. The additional expense to the funeral home for additional employees, building usage and perhaps equipment and merchandise, will add to the final total of your services.

Traditionally, funeral directors have taken care of all the details to free the family from the burden and laborious task of preparing and burying their deceased loved ones. They have invested years of study and practical application in the practice of funeral service. Their expertise to act on your behalf in preparing your loved one for final disposition is a profession in which few are willing to enter.

Your funeral services are limited only by your creativity. You are free to choose themes, colors, activities, locations, etc. for your funeral needs, just as you would a wedding. Your funeral director will see to all of the legal and preparatory aspects of laying your loved one to rest. He or she will coordinate all service details with ancillary personnel. These services provided by your funeral director free the family to concentrate on the needs of each other and plan the creative and personal side of their loved ones funeral.

When a young bride is preparing to wed, she is all consumed with the details of the glorious event. To date, this is the most important day of her life. Her wedding day pails however, at the birth of her first child and each one thereafter. The wedding is the beginning of her new life and the commencement of a new family. As she embarks and travels through her new life, she will one day come to the end of her existence. Her life will end and those she has created and loved will no longer have the privilege nor the influence of her association, the guidance of her loving council and experience, and most importantly, the unconditional acceptance and sacrifice of her enduring love. All physical association is lost at the death of this beloved family member, who throughout her life has sacrificed all that she was, and all that she had for her family's progress and happiness. At this juncture, one realizes how profound this loss actually is. Responsibilities for loving, charity, guidance and support must now be transferred from this loved one to others. Family members, as well as friends, are momentarily lost without her guiding light. One of trust, knowledge and unconditional loved toward all of her descendents must now be found for others to rely upon. In fact, when this woman first married, her responsibilities and circle of love were relatively small compared to those she has willingly created from that day forward. The day of her death transfers that responsibility to another and robs those left behind of her sweet and loving arms. This day has affected and changed many lives. It is a profound loss and mournful day for those she loved and for those who loved her.

Traditional Funerals

Many people confuse the term "Traditional" to mean that you must have the same funeral as your great grandmother.

Nothing could be further from the truth.

Traditional refers to the totality of the services performed by your funeral director, not a mundane repetition with merely a name change.

Perhaps you were a great benefactor to your city and gave them the land for a wonderful city park. If you did, perhaps you might want to have your funeral in that park under the beautiful cherry tree.

Perhaps you were fond of roses, and you want to have your funeral at the botanical gardens. Maybe you were a serious baseball fan, your funeral director could arrange with the city to host your funeral at the baseball diamond. Your options are endless, and you can personalize them as little or as much as you would like.

In San Diego, California I participated in a funeral where the decedent chartered a dinner cruise. She and her husband

honeymooned in San Diego and enjoyed their honeymoon dinner cruise so much that they decided to move and raise their family there. When pre-planning her funeral, she decided to treat her family to her fondest memory of beginning her life with her beloved husband in San Diego. She chartered a dinner cruise, and all of her family and close friends ate a wonderful meal, while cruising the San Diego shoreline, listening to a heartfelt eulogy and beautiful music. During the service, her guests were invited to share fond memories of the decedent.

Her guests were in beautiful attire; the flowers were amazing, the memories they shared were touching and their last experience with the decedent was relaxing, pleasant and appreciated.

Your funeral is only limited by your imagination (and funding of course); however, if you are creative, you can have a unique funeral that is not so terribly expensive. Create your funeral to express your love for your family and friends in such a way that they will remember it with fondness for years to come. Such a funeral is easy to accomplish, and unlike dreary funerals of the past, a personalized funeral may help move your family toward recovery in a healthier manner.

Think about the type of experience you would like your family and friends to remember on the day of your funeral. Inject your history and personality into the event. Provide them with one last personal moment with you before they lay you in your final resting place. Although they may be sad you are leaving them, they will appreciate and remember this final act of thoughtfulness and love with gratitude, and may find that they can adjust more easily to life without the benefit of your presence.

A good funeral is like a good wedding.

Both focus on the promise of your life.

The wedding hopes for successful accomplishment of that promise.

The funeral stands in review and appreciation of it.

CHAPTER 11

IN CONCLUSION

CONCLUSION

Because there are so many aspects to planning, funding and recovering from a death, my best advice is to prepare for the inevitable end of your life and that of those whom you love.

Prepare emotionally, prepare spiritually and prepare financially. If you will do these three suggestions, the death that you experience will be easier for all involved.

Remember, a funeral is for the living. Do all that you can in advance for those you will leave behind. They will no longer have the privilege of your presence among them for comfort, support or love. They will miss you greatly. Ensure that everything you could do to make your passing or the passing of a loved one easier on the survivors has been done.

Often during a Pre-Arrangement conference, people tell me, "Well, it's too late, nothing can be done." They give up on mending fences and bridges before their last breath has ended. The saddest part of my job is that I see the families of these people after they have passed on. The estranged children, aunts, parents and others are so devastated and long for one last moment to clear things up. Give them that chance.

One last thing and this is very important. If you feel that you have done wrong in your life, repair it now. Do not wait until next week, don't even wait until tomorrow. Pick up the phone or drive over to whomever you have hurt and repair the relationship. If there is one thing I know, it's that we never know when we are leaving this earth. Even if you think you do, you are only fooling yourself.

I see so much regret day after day and it could be erased and replaced with happiness if people would simply follow that little bitty suggestion.

God bless each and every one of you that are suffering the loss of a loved one.

Tracy Lee

General Price List

Services of our Funeral Directors and Staff

A. **Basic Services of Funeral Director and Staff** **$2,430**

This fee for our basic services will be added to the cost of the funeral arrangements you select. (A proportionate share of this fee is included in our charges for direct cremation, immediate burial and forwarding or receiving of remains.) Elements included in this fee are listed below:

- Arrangement interview and coordination of services.
- General clerical administration, bookkeeping and accounting fees.
- Securing vital statistics, recording the death certificate and other necessary permits.
- Coordination of service plans with clergy, cemetery, crematory or others involved with final disposition.
- Assistance with composing and placing obituary notices.
- Personnel available at your convenience, twenty-four/seven (24/7).
- Included in this fee as well are proportional fees for overhead expenses, professional licensing, legal and insurance fees, building and utility expenses, grounds upkeep and maintenance, real estate and other taxes, equipment, furnishings and inventory costs.

  ***Basic Services of Funeral Director and Staff fees are nondeclinable.**

B. **Additional Services of Funeral Directors and Staff**

- Coordination and direction of **funeral or memorial** service at a facility other than our funeral home during normal business hours. $95
- Coordination and direction of a **graveside service** at place of final disposition or immediate burial during normal business hours.
  (This charge does not include equipment used at the place of final disposition, cemetery fees, or gate fees.) $570
- Coordination and direction of **rosary or prayer** service at a facility other than our funeral home during normal business hours. $300
- Additional fee for **evening** funeral ceremony, memorial service, rosary, or prayer service at a facility other than our funeral home. $200
- Additional fee for **Sunday** funeral ceremony, memorial service, rosary, prayer service, viewing or visitation at a facility other than our funeral home. (If service is ending after 5:00 pm, evening fees shall also apply.) $300
- Additional fee for **Holiday** funeral ceremony, memorial service, rosary, prayer service, viewing or visitation at a facility other than our funeral home. (If service is ending after 5:00 pm, evening fees shall also apply.) $300

- **International/Cremation documentation preparation** assistance (priority request. Does not include document or filing fees) $295

C. **Use of Funeral Home Facilities**

- **Funeral Home facilities and staff for funeral or memorial service during regular business hours. $95**

Use of facilities and staff for viewing/visitation during regular business hours. (2 hour time allotment) **$95**

- Use of Funeral Home facilities and staff for rosary or prayer service during regular business hours. $300
- Additional fee for **evening** funeral ceremony, memorial service, rosary, or prayer service at our funeral home. $200
- Additional fee for **Sunday** funeral ceremony, memorial service, rosary, prayer service, viewing or visitation at our funeral home. (If service is ending after 5:00 pm, evening fees shall also apply.) $300
- Additional fee for **Holiday** funeral ceremony, memorial service, rosary, prayer service,viewing or visitation at our Funeral Home. (If service is ending after 5:00 pm, eveningfees shall also apply.) $300
- Ceremonial Washing and/or Dressing by family or appointed other during regular business hours. $415
- Use of video or sound equipment $195
- Refrigeration (maximum 72 hours, if available) $475

II. **Preparation of Remains**

D. **Embalming** **$650**

Except in certain special cases, embalming is not required by law. Embalming may be necessary, however, if you select certain funeral arrangements, such as a service with viewing. If you do not want embalming, you usually have the right to choose an arrangement that does not require you to pay for it, such as direct cremation or immediate burial. Our policy is that human remains will not be held at our facility pending final disposition arrangements beyond a 24 hour period from its arrival without being embalmed. If you have any questions regarding this policy, please feel free to contact the Texas Funeral Service Commission at P.O. Box 12217, Capitol Station, Austin TX 78711 or at (512) 936-2474.

E. **Other preparation Services**

Custodial care while sheltering remains (embalmed [unembalmed if refrigeration is available] per day after 72 hours) $200

- **Dressing and casketing only** (embalmed remains only) **$190**

- Reconstructive restoration when necessary (per hour) $20
- Special care for autopsied remains $150
- Post long bone donation $175
- Post organ, tissue, or science donation (does not include delivery of remains or donation fees to place of donation) $125
- Washing and disinfecting of unembalmed remains $300
- Dressing and/or casketing only (This charge applies to unembalmed remains, it does not include washing or disinfecting of remains) $190
- Hair cut, styling, or coloring (This charge is for Funeral Home staff, not professional cosmetologists, per hour) $79
- Hair cut, styling, or coloring (Professional Cosmetologist, per hour) as quoted
- Refrigeration (maximum 72 hours, if available) (TX Code #S181.4 preservation) $475
- Refrigeration (after 72 hours, per day, if available) $200
- Ceremonial Washing and/or Dressing by family or appointed other $415
- Pacemaker removal for purposes of cremation $179
- Cosmetizing (Embalmed remains only per hour) $79
-

F. **Transportation**

Unless otherwise noted, all transportation charges contained in this General Price List apply to local area only. Transportation in excess of 30 miles will be subject to additional charges of $2.00 per mile, per vehicle.

- **Initial transfer of loved one to funeral home** **$225**
- Funeral lead car/sedan (three hours or less, $150.00 per hour thereafter)$185
- Family Limousine (three hours or less, $150.00 per hour thereafter) $95
- Additional Limousine or contract Limousine (three hours or less, $150 per hour thereafter) $375
- **Funeral Coach** (three hours or less, $150.00 per hour thereafter) **$95**
- Pallbearer car (three hours or less, $150.00 per hour thereafter) $185
- **Flower/Service vehicle** (three hours or less, $150.00 per hour thereafter)**$95** This fee includes handling and arranging flowers at funeral home, church and graveside.
- Errand/Utility vehicle (message service, three hours or less, $150.00 per hour thereafter) $95
- Transporting remains to or from local common carrier (Texarkana TX only) $350
- Transporting remains to or from local crematory (commonly used by QCFH)$345
- Transporting remains to or from local medical examiner/coroner $350
- Daily Overland transportation service (does not include overnight accommodation charges or per mile fee) $350
- Additional fee to deliver flowers to home. $100

Transportation in excess of local 30 miles will be subject to additional charges of $2.00 per mile, per vehicle.

Bundle Discount

FORWARDING OF REMAINS to another Funeral Home **$2,145**

This charge includes:

- initial transfer of loved one to funeral home $225
- proportionate share of basic services of funeral director and staff $1,825
- transporting of remains to common carrier (Local Only) $350

Please note that this service does not include fees for other services including visitation, $2,400 before discount rites and ceremonies.

RECEIVING OF REMAINS from another Funeral Home **$2,015**

This charge includes:

- receiving loved one from common carrier (Local Only) $350
- proportionate share of basic services of funeral director and staff $1,825
- transporting loved one to local cemetery or crematory $345

Please note that this service does not include fees for other services including visitation, $2,520 before discount rites and ceremonies.

DIRECT CREMATION

In choosing a direct cremation for your loved one, it is important to realize that there are other fees associated with the cremation process that are not reflected in the following totals. These fees are listed separately as you have options on where and how to purchase them. These fees may include, but are not limited to an alternative container, crematory fees, obituary fees, cemetery property fees, cemetery gate fees, taxes, urns, death certificates, shipping fees and other services and merchandise.

If you want to arrange a direct cremation, an alternative container is required. alternative containers encase the remains and can be made of materials like fiberboard or composition materials (with or without an outside covering). The alternative container that we offer is a basic cremation container constructed of a plywood base. The crematory used by our funeral home does not allow the use of alternative containers made of non-ridged materials.

Direct Cremation does not include the use of facilities and staff for any visitation, funeralizing, memorializing, graveside services, graveside equipment, rites, ceremonies, merchandise or services.

Our charge for direct cremation includes:

- initial transfer of loved one to funeral home $225
- proportionate share of basic services of funeral director and staff $1825
- transporting of remains to crematory $345

Direct Cremation with container provided by purchaser. $2,395
(Please note that this total does not reflect charges for cash advance items, services or merchandise.)
Direct Cremation with alternative container provided by funeral home $2,655
(Please note that although this total includes the charge for an alternative container, it does not reflect charges for cash advance items, services or other merchandise you might select.)

Direct Cremation with casket selected from our funeral home Starting at $2,935
(Please note that this total does not reflect charges for cash advance items, services or other merchandise you might select.)

TRADITIONAL CREMATION SERVICE

Cremation with viewing and casket selected from our funeral home Starting at $4,470

- Initial transfer of loved one to funeral home $225
- Basic services of Funeral Home and staff $2120
- Embalming $650
- Other preparation of loved one $190
- Visitation $95
- Transportation of loved one to crematory $345
- Crematory fee $350

Cremation with viewing utilizing rental casket $5,214

- Initial transfer of loved one to funeral home $225
- Basic services of Funeral Home and staff $2120
- Embalming $650
- Other preparation of loved one $190
- Visitation $95
- Rental Casket $879
- Interior Insert $185
- Transportation of loved one to crematory $345
- Crematory fee $350
- Alternative container $175

FULL TRADITIONAL CREMATION SERVICE

Cremation with full services and casket selected from our funeral home Starting at $4,805

- Full Traditional Funeral Service $3,615
    - Initial transfer to loved one to funeral home
    - Basic services of Funeral Home and Staff

- Embalming
- Other preparation of loved one
- Visitation
- **Funeral Service or Memorial Service**

- Transportation of loved one to crematory $345
- Crematory fee $350

Extended sheltering of cremains (per day) $200
This per diem fee is charged beginning the 3rd day our facilities are used to shelter the cremains of your loved one.

Crematory Fee (Monday – Friday) $350

Familial observation of cremation (Not available with Direct Cremation) (limit 1 next of kin) $585

Alternative Container must be purchased in addition to Cremation fees. $175

Transferring and sealing of cremains into permanent Urn $75

Direct cremation is accomplished at the convenience of the Funeral Home. It does not allow for the participation or observation of others.
Immediate Burial **$2,145 - $24,620**
Our charges for an immediate burial include:

- initial transfer of loved one to funeral home $225
- proportionate share of basic services of funeral director and staff $1,825
- Local use of service utility vehicle for transportation to cemetery $95

Immediate burial with container provided by purchaser (does not include OBC)$2,620

Immediate burial with cardboard container (does not include OBC) $3,115

Immediate burial with casket selected from our funeral home 3,115 - $24,620

Immediate burial does not include the use of facilities and staff for any visitation, funeral, memorial or graveside rites, ceremonies or services. Immediate burial is accomplished at the convenience of the Funeral Home and does not allow for participation or observation of others.

IV. Merchandise

- Caskets
  (A complete list is available at the funeral home.) $795 - $22,000
- Immediate Burial, Alternative Cremation and Shipping Containers
  (A complete list is available at the funeral home.) $175-495
- Outer burial containers
  (A complete list is available at the funeral home.) $200 - $18,965

- Urns
  (A complete list is available at the funeral home.) $240 - $4,289
- Memorial Registers Starting at $50
- Second Memorial Register(Home Book) Starting at $50
- Door Wreath (Standard) Starting at $175
- Professional Photo Edit for Folders and Obit Starting at $195 hourly
- Graveside Water Service as quoted
- Graveside Umbrella Usage as quoted
- Acknowledgement cards (per 25) Starting at $25
- Memorial folders (per 50) Starting at $50
- Prayer cards (per 25) Starting at $50
- Crucifixes Starting at $25
- Flag cases Starting at $125
- Memorial video tribute (per 25 pictures) $195
- Additional copies of video tribute $25 each
- Memorial Portrait/Banner Starting at $175
- Memorial Canvas Portrait Study as quoted
- Memorial Candles (each) Starting at $15
- Bagpiper as quoted
- Pianist or Organist as quoted
- Vocalist (per location) as quoted
- Winged Tribute (1/2 dozen dove release) as quoted
- Balloon Release (with personal message) Starting at $275
- Personalized casket panels Starting at $150
- Custom Cap Panel Starting at $175
- Catering, per person Starting at $9.50
- Clothing Starting at $175
- Temporary Grave Marker $45
- Cremation Rental Casket Interior Insert $185
- Disaster Pouch $150
- Refrigeration Pouch $45
- Flowers as ordered
- Pall Bearer Gloves (per six pair) $65
- Use of church trucks or casket bier $665
- Cemetery Gate Fees (applies to most local rural cemeteries)$595 - $2,295
- Coffee Service during visitation Starting at $40
- Fresh Baked Cookie Service during visitation Starting at $40
- Pastry Service during visitation Starting at $45
- Sandwich Service during visitation Starting at $65
- Fruit Tray during visitation Starting at $65
- Meat Tray during visitation Starting at $65
- Cheese Tray during visitation Starting at $65
- Water Service during visitation Starting at $40
- Kitchen Usage(2 hours) $195

FUNERAL ESTIMATE SHEET

USE THIS WORKSHEET TO COMPARE THE COSTS BETWEEN FUNERAL HOMES TO DETERMINE WHICH ONE FITS YOUR BUDGET

	FUNERAL HOME		
	"A"	"B"	"C"
BASIC SERVICES OF FUNERAL DIRECTOR & STAFF	______	______	______
TRANSFER OF DECEASED TO FUNERAL HOME	______	______	______
EMBALMING OF DECEASED	______	______	______
OTHER PREPARATION OF BODY	______	______	______
USE OF FACILITIES & STAFF FOR VIEWING	______	______	______
USE OF FACILITIES & STAFF FOR CEREMONY	______	______	______
FUNERAL COACH	______	______	______
FAMILY CAR	______	______	______
OTHER CAR	______	______	______
CASKET	______	______	______
VAULT (OUTER BURIAL CONTAINER)	______	______	______
CREMATORY FEE	______	______	______
CREMATORY TRANSPORTATION FEE	______	______	______
DIRECT CREAMTION	______	______	______
IMMEDIATE BURIAL	______	______	______
RECEIVING OF REMAINS	______	______	______
SHIP OUT OF REMAINS	______	______	______
OTHER MERCHANDISE	______	______	______
OTHER MERCHANDISE	______	______	______
OTHER MERCHANDISE	______	______	______
OTHER MERCHANDISE	______	______	______
OTHER MERCHANDISE	______	______	______
OTHER MERCHANDISE	______	______	______
TOTAL	______	______	______

GLOSSARY OF TERMS

THE GLOSSARY OF TERMS IS INCLUDED TO HELP YOU UNDERSTAND THE LEGAL TERMS REGULATED BY THE FEDERAL TRADE COMMISSION.

GLOSSARY OF TERMS

Funeral Terminology

Arrangement Conference: A meeting with the funeral director at the funeral home to make funeral arrangements.

At-Need: The selection and payment of funeral services, interment rights, cemetery services and products at the time of death.

Casket (Coffin, Burial Case): A container fabricated of metal, wood, fiberglass or plastic, designed for the placement of human remains for burial.

Committal Service: The final section of the funeral service in which the decedent is entombed or interred.

Custodial Acceptance: The moment when the responsibility of care for your deceased loved one is passed from you to a licensed funeral director.

Eulogy: The article written and prepared for delivery at a funeral that honors the deceased. A eulogy is usually written and presented in a storytelling fashion.

Final Disposition: The last process for the remains - ground burial, entombment or cremation.

Final Rites: The funeral service.

First Call: The first visit by the funeral director to the place of death to remove the decedent and obtain pertinent information.

Funeral Arrangements: The final selection and purchase between the funeral home and family to complete the service and financial details of a funeral.

Funeral Procession: The procession of motor vehicles between the church and cemetery.

Funeral Service: The religious or other rites performed before final disposition of a deceased human body.

Graveside Service: A funeral that does not include a viewing, visitation or chapel service. A brief word is generally said by a friend or family member and perhaps a prayer at the cemetery. Usually lasts 15 to 20 minutes.

Hearse/Casket Coach: A motor coach designed and used to convey casketed remains from the funeral service location to the cemetery.

In State: A custom that presents deceased persons for viewing by friends and relatives either before or after the funeral service.

Memorial Service: A religious ceremony that is conducted in memory of the deceased without the remains present.

Obituary: A notice of death that contains biographical details of the deceased; usually a brief, factually based newspaper notice.

Open & Close: A service that opens (digs) the grave and closes (returns the earth back into) the grave. Also, provides the necessary equipment to safely lower the decedent into the grave. Equipment is provided for the safety and comfort of the attendees as well.

Pre-Arrangement: The selection of interment rights, cemetery services and products without respect to funding contracts.

Pre-Need: The selection and payment of interment rights, cemetery services and products before the time of death.

Register: A book made available to record the names of people visiting the funeral home to pay their respects to the deceased, as well as entering vital data on deceased (name, date of birth and death), name of officiant, place of interment, list of floral tributes, time and date of service, etc.

Service Car: A utility vehicle belonging to the funeral home or cemetery used to transport chairs, flowers, etc.

Traditional Funeral: A service that generally includes an arrangement conference with a licensed Funeral Director, visitation, funeral service, embalming, other care of the deceased, hearse, utility car, procession to the cemetery, committal service, and an open & close.

Viewing: A period of time when the deceased is available to be visited and seen by friends and relatives before or after the funeral service.

Visitation: An opportunity for friends and associates to visit the family and offer condolences.

Visitation or Viewing Room: A room in the funeral home where the body lies before the funeral service for people to view the deceased.

ABOUT THE AUTHOR

ABOUT THE AUTHOR

Tracy's heritage is deeply rooted in the Southern United States of America. She spent her youth running through the forests and swamps of Louisiana, and spent her teen years in the beautiful Rocky Mountains, along the Wasatch Front. This mix of cultures instilled a strong love for beauty, honor and nature in Tracy's heart.

As a teen, yearly visits to her grandmothers' homes helped her to realize the importance of family and tradition. Western influences brought into Tracy's life strong work ethics and an ardent appreciation for the arts.

As a young woman, Tracy resided in France. The beautiful architecture of the Cote D'Azur and rich treasures of L'artiste Renaissance were inspirational to her. Her visits to the beautiful grande maisons, palaces, chateaux, museums and bastilles of France brought an appreciation for architecture, liberty and art into her awareness.

Tracy married G. Michael Lee, a career military man, and they began their family. She worked at home as a daycare provider and enjoyed being able to love and inspire the children in her care.

When Michael retired from the military, he and Tracy started a photography business. Their business, Angel Shots, Inc. (www.AngelShotsPhotography.com) grew very fast, and they enjoyed many years creating wonderful portraits for their clients.

One afternoon while attending an art symposium in Colorado, Tracy decided she wanted to become an artist. She purchased the necessary tools and began to paint. Her first portrait inspired commissions before it was even completed. Within one month of pursuing her desire of becoming an artist, Tracy had been commissioned to paint for several others. Tracy has no official education in art or art techniques. She is completely self-taught and self-created.

While on tour in Las Vegas, Michael was approached by Frank Bare. He asked Michael about the paintings in his photography studio. Michael told him that his wife had painted them, and Frank Bare asked to contact Tracy. Frank Bare was the founder of the United States Gymnastics Federation and asked Tracy to become the official artist for the International Gymnastics Hall of Fame. Tracy joined the International Gymnastics Hall of Fame in 2009. She has had a lifelong appreciation of gymnastics and enjoys her association with the Hall.

Tracy Lee's work can be seen at her website www.AngelShotsPhotography.com. Her works for the International Gymnastics Hall of Fame can be seen at www.ighof.com. Tracy is also a board member of the Cass County Performing Arts Council.

In 1999, Tracy's grandmother, Amma Essie Zylks Harville, visited her family in Southern California. Unfortunately, Amma died during her visit. Tracy, her sisters and her mother went to the funeral home to help prepare her grandmother for travel back to the Southern United States for burial. That was the life changing experience that prompted Tracy to become a funeral director.

Tracy, Michael and their daughters have opened a funer al home in East Texas. Their website is www.QueenCityFuneralHom e.com. Their goals are to serve the people of the area in the way that they would want to be served, respectfully with dignity and love.In 1999, Tracy's grandmother, Amma Essie Zylks Harville, visited her family in Southern California. Unfortunately Amma died during her visit. Tracy, her sisters and her mother went to the funeral home to help prepare her grandmother for travel back to the Southern United States for burial. That was the life changing experience that prompted Tracy to become a funeral director.

Tracy, Michael and their daughters have opened a funeral home in East Texas. Their website is www.QueenCityFuneralHome.com. Their goals are to serve the people of the area in the way that they would want to be served, respectfully with dignity and love.

After becoming a funeral director, Tracy looked for information to help her clients recover from the sorrow of their grief. At first, she would recommend books written by educated grief experts, but found that on occasion, large scientific books were just too much for a grief stricken person to read and absorb. She continued her search for something easier for her clients to utilize and eventually began writing the articles herself. Tracy now writes a weekly bereavement article and a mid-weekly Grief Brief for well over 300 newspapers across the United States. She receives letters from her readers and is beginning a third column in response to these letters. If you would like to write Tracy, please feel free to do so at Queen City Funeral Home 421 Loop 236 Queen City Texas 75572, or email her at info@QueenCityFuneralHome.com. In addition to newspapers and magazines, Tracy offers her writings on her blog http://pushin-up-daisies.blogspot.com/.

Tracy and Michael have purchased an internet TV broadcasting station and will soon begin specialized programs focusing on recovering from bereavement and overcoming grief. Please feel free to check www.QueenCityFuneralHome.com for broadcast information and schedules.

Tracy and Michael are in the process of searching for a radio broadcast network to develop and implement a radio program where her readers may call in and ask their questions relating to their personal grief experiences and recovery. They feel that the open sharing of experiences will facilitate recovery for the newly bereaved and those suffering bereavement in isolation.

Tracy and Michael host an annual Womens Conference at Queen City Funeral Home. The conference focuses on women's issues. Past conferences have focused on fashion, health, beauty, preparedness, education, wealth, naturopathy and many more vital topics, regarding the lives and issues of women.

Tracy and Michael also host a live nativity at the funeral home each year. Holidays can be a difficult time for the bereaved. The live nativity gives grieving families and those within the community an opportunity to experience Christmas with those who understand the difficulties they are facing. Volunteers are invited to participate each year on their holiday Christmas Parade float and in the nativity as well.

Michael is a licensed Audioprosthologist, a hearing aid specialist, and offices in Queen City Funeral Home. Tracy and Michael believe in the importance of good health for their clients. In a proactive practice based on the philosophy of prevention, they offer free hearing screenings and consultations for their clients. Being able to hear during a vulnerable time, brings comfort and helps quell fears. For the bereaved, restoring the ability to hear assists in resocialization. Resocialization is a critical element in grief recovery.

And finally, our darling daughters have opened an internet store where they sell bracelets, necklaces and earrings. The profits from each sale are put into a fund, which helps fund infantile death costs. They have named their jewelry "Beaded Sentiments". They are also compiling a listing of free cemetery property across the nation to help families who are unable to afford property for purchase.

www.ingramcontent.com/pod-product-compliance
Lightning Source LLC
Chambersburg PA
CBHW051835090426
42736CB00011B/1814

* 9 7 8 0 9 8 9 4 4 4 7 5 0 *